Ego Strength

Betting on Myself

A true story of risk, resilience, and results

By Chuck Cuda

Ego Strength

Betting on Myself: A true story of risk, resilience, and results

ISBN Paperback: 979-8-89576-091-8
ISBN Hardback: 979-8-89576-092-5

Published by:

Acknowledgments

First and foremost, I would like to thank my wife, Annamarie, for being my partner in love and life. I cherish your love, loyalty, and devotion to me and our family. You have been by my side since I was just a young entrepreneur hanging Christmas lights for extra cash. You were one of the few who believed in me and stayed by my side through the most difficult period of my life. You never doubted that, together, we would make all our dreams come true. Thank you for always giving me the latitude, support, and ability to chase my visions and dreams, regardless of how unrealistic they seem. Your belief in me helps me believe in myself.

To my four incredible children—three lively boys and my beautiful daughter—thank you for being the light of my life. Your love, laughter, and endless energy inspire me every day. I see my greatest legacy in you, and your presence fills my world with joy and purpose.

A special thank you to my son Johnny, who took the initiative to help out and created his own "Eggo Strength" book cover, which can be found at the back of the book.

I want to thank my parents, who taught me the importance of family, what it means to be a husband and father, and instilled in me the entrepreneurial spirit that led to my many successes. My mother always saw my potential, and my father showed me the meaning of strength and perseverance. To my sister, you were always my biggest cheerleader and always believed in and supported everything I did in life and athletics. You always seemed more confused than I was if I failed or missed my goals.

I want to thank Uncle Frank for his unwavering support, always offering a silver lining and helping guide me through strategy and ideas in this book. His ability to step in with answers and structure in lay terms, and be a constant source of strength, has meant the world to me.

I want to thank my Uncle Paul, who first believed in me enough to give me an opportunity and then cared about me enough to not enable me, requiring me to use my ego strength to live up to my true potential.

To my friends and extended family, thank you for shaping me into the person I am today. Your quiet support and understanding, even when no words are spoken, have been invaluable—especially when dealing with someone who often thinks they can do anything.

To all of my employees, past and present, I appreciate the dedication and hard work you each put into your jobs. Together, we have built something important and special. I couldn't have done it without all of you.

Thank you to my lifelong friend Chris Rau. Your creative vision laid the foundation for the cover, capturing the eight traits of ego strength while reflecting the reality of our shortcomings. Your imagery brought the heart of this book into focus.

Thank you to Jo Rust for encouraging me to write the first manuscript, which consisted of 97 pages. Even if the content didn't make it to the final copy, it truly was the hardest part of the journey.

Thank you to Kathleen Sperduti for reigniting my desire to complete the project and making it fun and engaging. Without you, I don't think I would have gotten to the finish line.

Finally, I would like to acknowledge the role my faith has played in my journey. It gives me strength, reminds me of my values, and keeps me grounded.

Table of Contents

Introduction

What is Ego Strength?

It's not about arrogance or feeling superior to others. Ego strength is the capacity for self-awareness, resilience, and personal growth. The theory originates from American psychoanalyst Erik Erikson, who outlined eight components of ego strength: hope, will, purpose, competence, fidelity, love, care, and wisdom.

Your level of ego strength reflects your ability to look at yourself honestly and confront the aspects that no longer serve you or your highest purpose. It means being able to say, *"This isn't working—I need to change it."* It also requires taking full responsibility for your actions and choosing how you react to thoughts, emotions, and behavior at any given moment. Ultimately, it's about doing what's necessary to reach your full potential.

That is ego strength.

As I reflect on my journey, I marvel at the complexity of life. Like many others, my story has twists and turns, highs and lows, moments of triumph, and periods of struggle. My life has been anything but ordinary. This book is not just a memoir; it offers lessons in resilience, growth, and how to live a life of abundance by maximizing one's personal potential.

Born into a modest Italian-American family, my childhood was far from affluent. We weren't struggling, but fancy houses and flashy cars were distant dreams. I am deeply grateful to my parents for instilling the values of hard work, persistence, and standing on one's principles. Their resilience created a childhood steeped in culture, blending Italian traditions with the American dream—an experience that profoundly shaped my values and character.

Thanks to a high IQ, academic success came easily during my early years. I soon realized that education extends far beyond the classroom. I began absorbing lessons from experience—learning from both wins and setbacks—and understanding that true knowledge is often gained in life's most unpredictable moments.

One defining moment of my early adult life was my refusal to testify against friends involved in illegal online betting. Despite the legal and personal consequences, I would not compromise my principles. That choice, though costly, taught me what it really means to remain true to yourself—especially under pressure.

This decision ultimately led to jail time, which was a life-altering experience. I was forced to adapt quickly, survive in an unfamiliar environment, and, more importantly, confront myself. The greatest lesson from that chapter was learning to take personal responsibility. I had to accept that I alone was accountable for my choices. Only by embracing that responsibility could I begin to reclaim control and reshape my path.

Let's begin with the four foundational pillars that shaped my journey: Mindset, Planning, Execution, and Continuous Development.

Mindset is the way we think, the beliefs we hold, and the attitudes we adopt. It shapes our reality. I learned early on that a positive, growth-oriented mindset is essential for turning challenges into opportunities. The mind is powerful, and mastering it is the first step toward achieving greatness. In these pages, I'll share how I cultivated an unshakable mindset that helped me thrive in the face of adversity.

Planning is the structure behind success. A goal without a plan is just a wish. My own planning process—both in life and in business—has been the foundation on which I've built everything. A solid plan is a compass, especially in the chaos of uncertainty. Without one, you drift.

Execution is where dreams become reality. All the plans in the world are meaningless without action. From my early ventures to the complex world of commercial real estate and investments, my relentless drive has been a key factor. I've always had a hunger to do more, to be more. That energy is what fuels execution.

An often-overlooked element of execution is the company you keep. Our environment and relationships have a profound effect on our direction. I've learned that surrounding yourself with driven, positive, and supportive people can change the trajectory of your life. These relationships aren't just nice to have—they're essential.

Continuous self-development is a theme that runs through my entire life. For me, success is not a final destination. It's an ongoing journey of learning, evolving, and refining who you are. From reading and reflection to leadership training, emotional intelligence, and mentorship, I have prioritized personal growth. I believe that deeper self-awareness leads to better decisions, personally and professionally.

Tools like meditation and affirmations help me clear my mind and stay focused. These practices, when done consistently, bring clarity, energy, and even a sense of alignment. Growth also means putting ego aside. I regularly seek feedback, undergo behavioral assessments, and participate in coaching to better understand how I lead and how I live.

Another core driver in my life is alignment with personal values. Staying true to my core beliefs   especially when tested—has helped me make the right choices. For me, family is central. I've worked hard to maintain a balance between ambition and presence at home. This book is not just about financial success. It's about aligning your life with what truly matters and finding harmony between personal and professional fulfillment, even while building businesses and wealth. That same clarity around values extends to how I approach wealth building—grounded in purpose, but also informed by strategy and a willingness to adapt.

Wealth creation does not happen overnight and cannot happen with true velocity without scaling and selling assets. The mentality of *buy and hold* is a strategy that has worked to minimize returns and mitigate losses, but it's a tale as old as time. If you really want to maximize wealth acceleration, you must not only be willing and able to reassess your positions within your investments but also take emotion out of the investment strategy.

You must have a realistic outlook on the market, market cap, and your ability to grow your existing equity position within each existing asset, market, or industry. I left prison and had to start my career over from scratch, leaning on my knowledge from before jail, what I learned during my time inside, and adapting to a new set of circumstances upon my release to build the multi-million-dollar portfolio I now manage.

This book is a candid account of my life's journey—a narrative rich with lessons, insights, and strategies for personal and professional development. As you turn these pages, I invite you to walk with me through the real story—complete with the wins and the wounds. I hope my journey will challenge you to reflect on your own and offer you tools and insights to help you become the highest and best version of yourself.

Let's begin.

Chapter 1:
Adversity Equals Opportunity

Never in my life would I have imagined that I'd wind up in jail. It's not something you plan for, you know? I come from a proud, hardworking, middle-class Italian-American family from Kansas City, Missouri, with good morals, values, and a strong work ethic instilled in me as a kid. So why in the world would I go and mess things up by getting myself thrown in the slammer?

One word: Loyalty.

I was born an entrepreneur, a dreamer, and a high-functioning visionary. I've always had high energy levels and a need to perform. As a kid in school, I never needed to make an effort in class. I qualified as a "gifted child" and was enrolled in an educational program for gifted children at a young age. I recall my mom getting so mad at me because I wasn't getting high enough test scores or straight A's. She felt like I wasn't applying myself and that I wouldn't make anything of myself in life if I didn't focus and perform at school. It came from a place of love, of course, as she only wanted what was best for me. But, because my brain needed different forms of stimulation than were offered, I would get bored. The subjects weren't intriguing enough, and the work wasn't challenging enough for me. The academic challenges didn't excite me. However, when presented with a real hands-on challenge in life, I was intrigued and consequently thrived.

I had a pretty "normal" childhood. It was just me, my older sister, and my mom and dad. My dad was my first role model, and much of what I apply in my roles as husband and father, I learned from him. Just as he was never too tired to play catch with me when I was a kid, despite long hours at the restaurant, I make it a point to never be too tired to spend time with my own kids, no matter how long a day I have.

I can honestly say that I inherited my drive and entrepreneurial spirit from my father. My parents were in the restaurant business their entire lives, and my father played a major role in teaching me the value of determination. At one point, my parents had five restaurants, but my father's vision was to franchise or have a chain of restaurants across the city. He was always trying to expand by opening more stores, but suffered multiple setbacks, including fires in three of his locations.

The first fire happened before I was born. A homeless person tried to stay warm by starting a fire in the stairwell of the building where his restaurant was located, resulting in the entire building catching fire. The second happened when a grease fire in another restaurant in the same strip center as my dad's restaurant destroyed the entire building because there were no firewalls in place. The third was an electrical fire involving a steam table that blew up due to a faulty breaker. Unfortunately, my dad's restaurants were not adequately insured to allow him to bounce back from multiple incidents.

As a kid, I blamed the fires and the lack of insurance for my parents' inability to continue to grow the business. As an adult with multiple successful businesses of my own, I now understand that my dad was not only underinsured but also undercapitalized. Additionally, he lacked the team and structure necessary to maintain his brand's integrity, especially when faced with unforeseen challenges, like the fires.

Still, my dad is one of the most resilient people I know. He always took a licking with every setback, kept on ticking, and stayed positive! Eventually, my parents decided to focus on just one restaurant and made a good living from it by putting all their time and effort into that location. Like many kids whose parents run a restaurant, I started working in my parents' restaurant at the age of 12.

While working there, I watched and learned from my father about business management and how to be structured and organized both personally and professionally. The greatest lesson I learned from watching my dad had less to do with business success and more to do with success in general. From my dad, I learned persistence. Watching his persistence despite numerous setbacks inspired me as a child. It taught me to be relentless in pursuit of my dreams, no matter the challenges.

As a child, my hobbies included sports and drawing. I have always enjoyed and been pretty good at drawing. I'd often draw pictures of baseball players or other sports figures. Pencil drawings have always been my go-to. It's what I enjoy most. When it came to sports, baseball was my passion, and it turned into more than just a pastime as I got older. My dad was my first coach and instilled in me a love of the game. He pushed me to expect more from myself, and that true improvement comes with practice and development, both inside and outside the lines.

My Uncle Paul was perhaps the second biggest mentor in my life after my father. He was someone who had successfully grown and scaled a business, and his kids were substantially younger than I was, so he and I were close as I grew up. I even helped him coach one of my younger cousins' baseball teams, so I could spend more time learning from him while still passing down baseball skills and knowledge to my cousin and his teammates. We developed more than an uncle/nephew relationship. It was more akin to a mentor/mentee relationship. I felt the security of knowing that in addition to my mother and father, I had my uncle, upon whom I could rely in good times and in bad.

I looked up to Uncle Paul as a husband, father, and businessman. I wanted to spend as much time as I could with him, and loved that he seemed to want to mentor me as much as I wanted to learn from him. Loyalty is a strong value in my family and in most Italian families, and my loyalty to Uncle Paul was unwavering. I felt his loyalty was as strong, but time would prove me wrong. Still, through my childhood and adolescence, the times I spent learning from him are some of my best memories.

Oddly enough, another aspect of sports that I enjoyed as a kid was gambling on the games. My family unintentionally started me on the path of gambling that would later cause me so much trouble. By the age of ten, I was attending dog and horse races with my family to the point where I could read the program schedules. I wasn't officially allowed to make bets, but I would choose the winners, and my dad or grandfather would collect the winnings on my behalf. Gambling on the races was a fun pastime for my family; they couldn't have known that it would be the start of a dangerous addiction for me as I moved into my teens.

For me, gambling matched well with my competitive nature.

Betting with buddies at school provided an adrenaline rush that was comparable to actually competing in a sport. By the age of 15, I had expanded to blackjack and playing craps. My friends and I would play in social and friendly settings for relatively low stakes. That started to change when I was 16, and I managed to get my hands on a convincing fake ID. I took that ID and went to Vegas with friends to do nothing but gamble. Once, when I was all of 17, my best friend, Joe Strada, and I played craps at a casino while carrying our baseball uniforms and cleats in a bag as we were heading out the door to one of our high school tournament games being held in Las Vegas. I won $3,000, slipped into uniform, showed up late to the pre-game warmups, and then pitched a one-hitter. I felt invincible.

As part of my education in becoming a man, my father taught me the traditional values he believed in. One of those was the importance of being able to support your family. He bought my sister a car, but I was expected to earn the money to buy my own. So, I took the challenge! I started a seasonal business hanging Christmas lights in the neighborhood and managed to pull in $20,000 over a two-month period. That should have been enough for a teenager. For me, it just fueled my desire for more.

When I was in college, I'd bet $400 or $500 on a college football game, then work at my dad's restaurant for $12 an hour the next day. Gambling gave me a rush. I tried to convince myself that it was a good way of supplementing my income. I wanted more–more money, more vacations, more things. Nicer things that I couldn't afford on $12 an hour working at my dad's restaurant.

So, I kept gambling, chasing the big win. Unfortunately, the numbers just never added up. Instead of a get-rich-quick scheme, I couldn't even make enough money to pay the VIG! (VIG stands for vigorish, also known as "juice" in sports betting. It's the fee a bookmaker charges for accepting a gambler's bet).

After high school, I attended an NCAA Division II school and played baseball there for a year. Then, I transferred to a junior college and played baseball there until I threw my arm out. I chose not to have surgery. To be honest, I was getting to a point in my life where I really just wanted an out so I could start making money. The injury provided me the perfect excuse not to play 40 hours of baseball per week. After receiving my associate's degree from junior college, I went to the University of Missouri at Kansas City for two years and majored in economics.

Around this time, my social, friendly gambling hobby had turned into a full-blown gambling addiction. By the time I turned 21 and could openly gamble without the need for a fake ID, I would routinely skip class to go to the casino to gamble or to the local dog track for parimutuel betting. At night, I would play PartyPoker, which was online poker. It was legal then, but has since been ruled illegal in the U.S., and all online cash games have been taken down. I was actually pretty good at online poker. I would win enough to supplement the other losses and countless hours spent at the local casinos gambling, which ultimately led me to fall 3 hours short of graduating with my economics degree. The school said I could walk at graduation with my class if I completed the 3 hours I needed over the summer, but I felt it was unfair to those who had actually met the graduation requirements. Plus, I knew I wasn't going to complete the hours needed. I was done.

It was the early 2000s. I was in my twenties and trying to figure out my life path going forward, which looked like joining my Uncle Paul's local brokerage in commercial real estate. He hired me as an intern. I was excited about the job and looked forward to learning about the commercial real estate brokerage business from him. Uncle Paul made a point to try to implement structure with me by enforcing policies like docking my paycheck if I arrived late, unshaven, or not dressed to his professional standards. I now feel that he was too hard on me, but back then, I just wanted to make him proud.

I quickly learned that I was a perfect fit for the world of commercial real estate. I became the number one salesperson in the company within two years at the age of 24, making well over $100,000 a year in commissions, forging relationships in the community, and perhaps most importantly, brokering millions of dollars in transactions for my uncle's business. By age 26, I was transacting deals for Walgreens and McDonald's and even landed a multi-million dollar deal with Hendrick's Automotive on a cold call. When I picked up their National Real Estate Director from the airport after he flew in from Charlotte, North Carolina, he was baffled at how young I was. This was a testament to how well my uncle had trained and mentored me, but it was also reflective of my growth, talents, and skill set.

If only that had been enough.

Since I have such a compulsive personality, I was getting more and more involved in sports betting at the same time. Back then, sports betting was illegal. In fact, any kind of online betting was illegal, but a couple of buddies of mine knew (or thought they knew!) their way around the system and were bookmakers taking bets from people like me. I would bet on professional or college sports, including baseball, football, and basketball. It could be any game with a line, even an unknown team that wasn't being shown on television, and I'd bet on it. It didn't matter; it was about the action.

Betting was fun and exhilarating.

It channeled my love for competition and gave my mind the opportunity to use analytics, which, I convinced myself, gave me an advantage. As any gambler knows, you can try and convince yourself as much as you want, but in reality, you never truly know what you're going to get unless you're in on fixed bets. I was never involved in the bookmaking side of things, but I had a good time placing bets and winning some money here and losing a lot there.

I eventually had to face the facts and admit to myself that I had a problem. I joined Gamblers Anonymous and attended meetings to try to kick my gambling addiction. Unfortunately, I still didn't quite understand just how bad things had gotten.

Let me explain: When I attended my first few meetings, some of the stories I heard from other attendees were so bad that I felt I didn't really have much in common with them. I hadn't gambled nearly as much money or lost as much in my life as they had. In fact, I didn't really feel I had that much of a problem at all until I overestimated my ability to control myself at the casino and lost more than just money one weekend in Vegas.

One of my lowest points was losing over $10,000 at the wedding of my best friend, Paul Guastello Jr., or as we call him, PJ, in Las Vegas. I showed up at the casino with $5,000 in my pocket and a vow to spend only that much, win or lose.

You know where this is going.

I didn't win. In fact, I was down $8,000. In my refusal to lose, I skipped the rehearsal dinner and ended up with additional credit card advances and losses that exceeded $10,000. I didn't sleep for 28 hours straight. By the time I realized I needed to get out of the casino, I knew I wouldn't be attending my best friend's wedding either.

Instead, I borrowed $100 from a friend, hopped in a cab, and took the first flight out, leaving behind my luggage and golf clubs. There were no remaining direct flights to Kansas City when I arrived at the airport, so I told the booking agent to give me the first flight out of Vegas, which was to Dallas/Fort Worth. When I landed, there were no more flights out to KC until the following morning. I had to sleep in the airport and wait for my flight home, which gave me time to reflect on what had just happened. I came to grips with the reality that my problems weren't as bad monetarily as some of my fellow Gamblers Anonymous members' problems, because I didn't have access to the same kind of money, not because I wasn't as compulsive. I didn't even tell my parents until I landed, and when I did, I felt disgusted.

Then I began to take recovery seriously.

I've thought a lot about what makes gambling so addictive to me. What most likely led to my gambling addiction is that, behaviorally, I'm a compulsive individual. When I'm committed to something, I'm *committed*! If I'm in, I'm *all in*! I'm going hard or I'm not going at all. This is true for commitments that may be good for me and for those that may be bad for me. My challenge is to direct this compulsion in the right direction.

In November 2009, the United States Federal Bureau of Investigation commenced an investigation into a major case of illegal gambling operations valued at $3.5 million. In connection with that investigation, a grand jury was established in the United States Court for the Western District of Missouri. This case investigated and targeted several of my friends who were bookmakers on the sports betting scene at the time. The investigation included sports betting activities in which I had partaken.

I received a subpoena to testify in front of the grand jury on August 6th, 2009, and was called as a grand jury witness. Rather than testify, I asserted my Fifth Amendment right of the U.S. Constitution not to testify and incriminate myself so that I would not have to provide evidence against my friends. I was caught between a rock and a hard place. What do you do? Testify against your friends, landing them in even more trouble, or remain loyal and risk going to the slammer for contempt of court? One of the lessons of my Italian-American culture and upbringing is the importance of loyalty and silence; these are values instilled in childhood. Despite the personal sacrifice, I was not going to talk.

Eleven witnesses asserted their Fifth Amendment right, refused to testify, and were held in civil contempt of court. I was one of them, which meant I was going to jail for up to eighteen months, which I already knew was coming.

Choosing to assert my Fifth Amendment right and not testify was not a decision that I came to lightly. My career in commercial real estate was taking off, and jail was going to be a major setback. I wasn't too concerned about that, though, as I knew I'd have a job waiting for me with my uncle when I got out, making the decision a little more palatable.

Then, there was the effect on my family. My father knew something was up and that I was involved in the case. I remember my dad telling me when I was younger and betting on games or going to the local dog track that if I kept it up, I'd end up in jail: a real Nostradamus, my dad. My mother was obviously very disappointed and worried about me, but I assured her that I'd be fine.

This was the second time that the federal prosecutor for the Western District of Missouri investigated and targeted sports betting in Kansas City, Missouri. The irony is that such activity is now completely legal, and people spend time doing it all day worldwide. Even back then, there were sports betting bookies all over the country taking bets. There was also Bovada™, which is an online sports betting site that still exists. The decriminalization of sports betting quickly spread across the United States in 2018, just 9 years after I was sent to jail. The case I was caught up in was a targeted investigation into "organized crime" in Kansas City, Missouri. They were clearly targeting a specific group of people and made the case out to be more than it was.

In United States Federal Court, if you invoke your Fifth Amendment right against self-incrimination and refuse to testify, you may be granted immunity from prosecution. That means that anything you say cannot be used against you in a criminal case, effectively eliminating the risk of self-incrimination. As a result, your right to refuse to testify is removed, since there is no longer a concern that your testimony could incriminate you.

Once the possibility of self-incrimination is removed, the judge orders the witness to testify. If the witness at that point continues to refuse to testify, the witness is in contempt of court and can be sent to jail until they comply with the Court's order to testify. If the witness continues to refuse to testify, the Court conducts what they call a "Show Cause" hearing, where the witness appears in front of the judge to show cause as to why they did not testify and why they should not be sent to jail for contempt.

This is where your attorney lists all the reasons why you shouldn't be held in contempt and sent to jail. In my case, my lawyer argued that I had no criminal record or prior infringements; I had financial obligations like house payments to make, which would go into default if I was in jail; never in the history of the United States had someone who had placed a bet on sports been sent to jail for this reason, etc. My hearing was scheduled for October 5th, 2009. Some of my friends involved in this case had already had their show cause hearings and had already been sent to jail.

Since I already had some friends on the inside, I kind of knew what to expect, so I wouldn't say that I was particularly nervous about the whole procedure that lay ahead. I was more relieved that the anticipation would finally be over. Jimmy, a family friend who had been on the inside, was let out because his brother had been diagnosed with and was dying of brain cancer. He was released so he could see his brother before he passed. While out, he gave me a rundown of what to expect and what to wear when going in, since they'd be taking certain items off me.

Going into the hearing, you're allowed to have certain people with you in the courtroom, like your parents, other family members, or friends. Standing outside the courtroom, waiting to go in, I told my mom to stay outside because I knew it would be a lot harder on her than it would be on me. Witnessing your son being sentenced to jail is not something that a mother should have to go through. I basically said goodbye to my parents outside in the hall before I went in; we all knew what the outcome was going to be.

My hearing lasted all of five minutes, after which I was cuffed by U.S. Marshals and put on a bus to Leavenworth CCA Detention Center. I was sentenced to up to 18 months in jail, and the judge told me I held the keys to my cell.

Once you get to jail, you first have to go to medical. You're put through some tests to make sure you're in good health before going into the general population. While awaiting test results and cell block assignment, you wait in a medical holding pod. My friend Jimmy had been sent back to jail and had to reclear medical. When I walked into the medical center, I saw him sitting there, watching a Monday night football game between the Packers and the Vikings. I asked him, "Who do you have?" I was joking, kind of.

The holding pod where I was assigned was a 7-by-10-yard room with bunk beds, one-inch-thick mattresses, pillows as supportive as a Sunday newspaper, one metal toilet, and one metal sink shared by two men. I was kept on a 20-hour lockdown until assigned to my cell block. Once I cleared medical, after a few days, I was assigned to my new "home."

A pod that had over 100 inmates.

Walking in, I ran into another buddy of mine, Tommy Cascone. When he spotted me, he ran up to me and said, "*Man, I'm so happy to see you here!*" I definitely wasn't as happy to see him. Another buddy of ours was assigned to the same pod a few weeks later. In that pod, I was in a

10-man cell; there were five sets of bunk beds, one metal picnic table bolted to the ground, one toilet - visible for all to see - a sink, and ten people, nine of whom were convicted felons, and me. There were all kinds of men in there with criminal records as long as my arm. Everyone appears a bit on edge while evaluating each other to see who's a threat and who isn't. The atmosphere was very tense at times.

Having slept in a room with nine other men who had committed crimes of murder and drug trafficking is a haunting memory, not one of my fondest. If something went wrong in there or someone had a beef, let's just say there wasn't going to be a pillow fight.

One source of tension at times was that Leavenworth CCA is a Federal Holding Facility, meaning that people in different pods were either awaiting their sentences, a transfer to another facility, or their final destination after sentencing. Everyone had "papers" that showed their conviction, except for our group of "contempt inmates." We didn't have conviction papers because we hadn't been convicted of a crime— we were incarcerated for contempt of court, not a criminal conviction.

This made things difficult because everyone would ask you what you were in for to determine who they could and could not trust. Our group, without papers, led to many arguments because no one believed us when we told them that we were in for contempt of court. They suspected us of being planted as snitches to get information from them, which added to the level of distrust, hostility toward us, and stress.

In general, we were on lockdown for 16 hours a day and allowed only one hour of recreation time during the day. We only had one visit per week, and only three people could visit at a time for 30 minutes. We would communicate through glass and by talking through the two-way phones; no contact visitation. I had a lot of time to sit and think.

Something that allowed me more time out of my cell was being the pod porter. I would clean up the pod's common area, earning me an extra meal whenever I wanted. I almost never wanted it because the food was so bad. The only extra meal I wanted was Frosted Flakes™ with real milk instead of powdered milk mixed in a five-gallon drum.

One day, another inmate grabbed my extra tray of food. This didn't sit well with me as I was so looking forward to having a little "treat." I called out his name to get his attention, but he just kept walking, acting like he couldn't hear me. I impulsively got up, walked up behind him, and knocked the tray out of his hands. I say impulsively because this was not planned. I wasn't planning a fight. I didn't even have my shoes on. The moment I did that, I knew a fight was coming, so I quickly ran into my cell and grabbed my shoes to put them on. He followed me in and started punching me as I was putting my shoes on, and I did the best I could to hold my own against this criminal. It felt like we were going at it for 20 minutes, but it was probably more like 45 seconds. The only time I ever got into a fight in prison was over a bowl of Frosted Flakes™!

Spending Thanksgiving in prison was my rock bottom. I had been in jail for eight weeks by then, and I knew I had to make a change. To give the correctional officers the day off, we were on a 23-hour lockdown. We were allowed out of our cells for an hour to make phone calls to friends and family. Holidays like Thanksgiving, Easter, and Christmas are big affairs for Italian families, and while my family was celebrating together, I sat alone in a jail cell with a bologna sandwich. That was, as they say, my "Aha!" moment.

For the first eight weeks, I found myself sitting in my cell, blaming my friends for getting caught, blaming the prosecutor for prosecuting a victimless crime, and blaming the judge for putting me in jail, not for a crime but for not ratting on my friends. It's so easy to be the victim. My circumstances were not my fault, but instead, the fault of others. If that were true, then I did not control the outcome of my own life. I would lack any control over my circumstances.

And then, it hit me.

I was in jail not because of my friends' actions, not because of the prosecutor, nor the judge - I was in jail because of me.

I chose to gamble.

I chose to involve myself in this conduct.

I chose to subject myself to this risk.

Once I admitted this, I was able to take responsibility and be accountable for my actions. I realized that I was in control. This realization enabled me to make changes in my life. I understood that my life was not controlled by others. And with that control, I understood that I could direct my life.

Being the victim is easy. It's lazy.

Being in control meant shifting the work to me, but it allowed me to choose success or failure.

I'm the kind of person who struggles just to sit still and do nothing. I had to find ways of keeping myself occupied so I wouldn't get bored to the point of losing my mind. Thanks to my entrepreneurial wiring, I also made a bit of money on the side, as you can only get a certain amount of money sent from the outside to your commissary.

At one point, someone in our case unlocked his cell, testified, and was able to go home to his family. Then the Feds put a separate order that none of us could be assigned to the same pods. They wanted us to be as uncomfortable as possible in the hope that we'd crack and slip information. I was transferred to a different pod and put in a 3-man cell.

The food in CCA was absolute garbage. I went in weighing around 210 pounds, and when I got out five months later, I weighed 176 pounds. It's like partaking in a version of *The Biggest Loser* without personal trainers, healthy food, or proper gym equipment. We had to fill empty soda bottles with water, throw them into pillowcases, and use them as weights! Bodyweight exercises like pushups, pullups, and human resistance were our main ways to get in shape and work our muscles.

I did, however, learn how to get better food for myself by using my creative talent to draw pictures of other inmates' families and loved ones for 20 bucks. Everyone on the inside is always looking for things to send back home as gifts, so this was one way for me to both keep myself occupied, have a creative outlet, and make some money. I'd create maybe 8 to 10 drawings a week.

Let's face it: I had plenty of free time, so I decided to make use of it. Sometimes, instead of money, I traded drawings for books people sent me from the outside. Books were hard to come by in jail, so this was my way of getting more reading material. When I wasn't drawing or reading, I'd play chess, spades, or basketball with the other guys.

I was done shying away from taking responsibility for my mistakes. I had landed myself in prison as a consequence of my actions in the past. My situation was all on me, and that time really gave me the opportunity to consider what I wanted to do with my life.

People often land themselves in less-than-favorable situations in life through no one's fault but their own. They refuse to own up and take responsibility for their own actions. Life is a series of choices made on a day-by-day basis. If you think about it, you can choose to go in a different direction at any moment. You're not a tree rooted in place, unable to move. Everything in life is a choice. Not making a change is a choice. Even when we don't necessarily have a say in what happens to us, we do choose how we respond to it.

I accepted my punishment and did my time, knowing that this was just a bump in the road and that I'd have a job at my uncle's company when I got out. When you zoom out a bit, I really wasn't in that bad of a situation. Sure, being in jail sucked. But there are worse places to be.

The trajectory of your life is determined by how you choose to view adversity. We all have difficult situations we have to deal with in life, to varying degrees. Yes, you might think that the CEO in his Ferrari couldn't possibly have gone through what you have to get to where he is. The thing is, you never know. I know millionaires, like my friend PJ, who grew up pedaling salvaged freight out of the trunk of his car.

You look at some people and think that they must've had it easy in life. They were probably born into a rich family. They were born with a silver spoon in hand, part of the lucky sperm club.

The truth is, the path to success has been paved with many obstacles, trials, and tribulations. I never dreamed of landing in jail. My dream was to make it big in the business and entrepreneurial world. There I was, with a choice to make: blame others and play the victim card, or change my situation.

That's what failure and adversity are: opportunities for you to learn and grow as an individual so you do better the next time around.

As the famous quote from the Rocky movie goes, "It ain't about how hard you hit. It's about how hard you can get hit and keep moving forward."

That's how resilience is formed. It stems from being given the opportunity to work through difficult situations and learn as much as possible from them, so you can develop into a better version of yourself.

We can't compare one person's experiences with another's. No two people experience life or situations the same. How I think and how you think are two very different things. The way I see the sky and the way you see that exact same sky may be very different.

As I said, I had a lot of time to read and think. I could've sat in my little cell and spent my time harboring resentment against the people I didn't testify against out of loyalty. But again - my choice. I could've wallowed in the fact that I didn't listen to my dad when I was a kid, and continued gambling, and the fact that it landed me in custody. I could've felt anger toward myself, but you have to ask, to what end? How would any of these options have helped me in any way? It wouldn't have been a productive use of my time.

So, I focused on bettering myself, continuing personal growth, and pursuing a better version of myself. Reading books and educating myself was a far better use of time than sitting around doing nothing. I chose to focus on the positives. There was no access to alcohol, tobacco, or takeouts, so my body was able to detox in a sense, and I lost weight, which was a positive. We did make prison wine sometimes, though. For those of you who don't know, the way you make prison wine or "hooch" is you take the fruit off the food tray you get in jail, mixed with some Hawaiian punch and some source of yeast you get from your commissary, and then put it in a bag in under your bunk in a dark place and let it sit so it can ferment and turn some of those sugars into alcohol.

I had some choices to make. Choices regarding what I wanted to do with my life and the goals I had for myself.

I wanted to start a family and comfortably provide for them.

I wanted to do more than just work for a boss. I wanted to be the boss and make a positive difference in the lives of others.

There was so much I still wanted to do with my life, and prison was really, probably, the best thing that could've happened to me because it forced me to take a step back so I could gain some perspective on my life. I didn't just want to change myself; I wanted to promote change in others.

Sometimes, life places you in situations you'd rather avoid to give you a clearer perspective. It helps you understand who you want to be, who you don't, and where you want to go, or not go. Ultimately, it's up to you to learn the lesson and turn it into something positive for the future.

Chapter 2:
The Best Revenge is Massive Success

I was released on February 18, 2010, after serving just over four and a half months in prison. During that period, I had a lot of time to think about where my life was heading and what I wanted to do going forward. It might be hard to believe, but I'm incredibly grateful for that experience. Prison taught me personal responsibility, accountability, and self-determination. It's funny how losing my freedom actually taught me how to take control of my life.

Following my low point on Thanksgiving, I decided to do the inner work and grow as an individual. I took responsibility for my decisions, got in physical and mental shape, and lost weight by committing to physical activity. I also spent a lot of time planning for the changes I would make in my life upon my release. Rather than feeling that my life had been derailed by being locked up, I was excited about starting a new chapter. Digging up the past only muddies up the present. With this new understanding, I looked forward to getting back out there to attain the goals I had set for myself.

I wanted financial success to support my wife and a family. I didn't want to worry about money and have to constantly hustle to make ends meet. One of the comforts that helped me stay positive was the expectation that I had a job secured at my uncle's company, where I would be able to step back into my previous successes.

When my time in jail was up, I left a changed man. I hadn't anticipated making strong friendships with criminals who had committed crimes far more serious than contempt of court, but that was just another lesson learned. Some of those relationships would prove to be pivotal in my journey moving forward. In others, I would be the one fortunate enough to lend a helping hand over the years.

About a week after I got out, I met my uncle over lunch to discuss the plan for returning to my job with the company. Unfortunately, things didn't go according to plan. I had left prison thinking that the biggest challenge of my life was behind me. I didn't know that an even bigger blow was coming my way from one of the people I admired most.

My uncle informed me that the situation had changed while I was away, and he no longer felt I would be a good fit for his company.

This news was a punch to the gut. The financial loss was a factor, sure, but I knew I would find work elsewhere. It wasn't about the money for my uncle, either. Although I had been his top salesman for three years before I went to jail, he now worried about how rehiring me would negatively impact his reputation and perception in the community as an individual and as a businessman.

When I was deep into my gambling addiction, my uncle once said to me, "If you hang around people who walk with a limp, sooner or later, you'll walk with a limp, too." I realized that day that in his eyes, I had become the guy with the limp, and my own uncle saw me as a liability. The true pain came from my feelings of betrayal from someone I trusted, relied upon, and admired. My uncle was my mentor and role model. Honestly, this was a far more challenging blow to overcome than being sent to prison. It wasn't a blow delivered by strangers, such as the prosecutor or the judge; it was a blow delivered from someone within my inner circle, from whom I expected loyalty.

The first thing I did after that meeting was call my parents to find out whether they knew about my uncle's decision. My uncle is the husband of my mom's sister, and they were close, so I believed my parents had to have known about it in advance. Still, they acted shocked at the news, or perhaps they really didn't know about it.

It took some time to process the rejection and betrayal. Several months earlier, I had chosen loyalty to my friends, and because of that choice, I went to prison. Then, my mentor, my uncle, *my family* chose not to be loyal to me when I needed him most.

This was my first real test on the outside. I could see it as a sign that I had made the wrong choice in choosing friendship and loyalty over saving my own hide, and give up before I even began, or I could put all the changes I had made in prison into practice in the real world.

With every challenge comes opportunity.

I chose to see this as an opportunity. It didn't happen overnight. I needed some time to process before I was ready to move on and start fresh. I questioned what our relationship had ever really meant to him.

Obviously, I was expendable.

Was I merely viewed as a talent, where my skill set was meant for driving revenue to his company? I thought back to all the times I felt he was showing tough love: docking my pay if I showed up late or not dressed to the nines with a half-Windsor tie, expecting more of me than from others, and I began to see it in a new light. I thought he was mentoring me to grow in the business. Now, I wasn't so sure. He was happy to have me around when times were good, but he would not be there for me when the chips were down.

He abandoned me in my time of need.

The road to attaining my goals may have gotten a little longer and steeper, but with strengthened resilience and newfound control, I rose to the challenge and began the climb.

This was yet another turning point for me, and it's important to be clear about a few things. My uncle's decision to cut business ties with me was his personal choice, but it was a consequence of my own actions, and I own that. My poor behavior had cost me my freedom and then cost me my career with my uncle's firm. More importantly, it had cost me my relationship with my uncle, at least in the short term.

After the pain and disappointment subsided, I wanted vengeance. Not the kind where I ruin his life or his business, but the kind where I become so successful in my own business that he would regret ever letting me go. I have learned over the years that my success doesn't have to mean taking away someone else's, but I did want to show my uncle that, from a business standpoint, letting me go was the biggest business mistake he would ever make.

I made a list of everyone I knew in the commercial real estate brokerage community who had an office or was the broker of record for their respective office. My good buddy, whose dad was the managing director at Global Commercial Real Estate Services (CBRE), also had his own brokerage company, so I called and met with him. I basically called everyone I'd ever done deals with and set up meetings. I wanted to make sure I could meet with people face-to-face to explain exactly what had happened and what they could expect of me going forward. I wanted to be upfront with them about my past situation because I'd learned many lessons and wasn't about to start off on the wrong foot by not being totally transparent. I owned my past and needed to be sure that it wouldn't be a barrier to any potential business relationships in the future.

After relentless pursuit, a local real estate company offered me a job as a property manager. Although I was grateful for the offer, I declined. I know you may be thinking, *"What the hell? You were looking for a job, got offered a job, then declined it?"* I did, and I would again.

My wife Annamarie asked me the same questions. We married on June 9, 2010, less than four months after my release. Annamarie was making decent money working at Beauty Brands as an esthetician, which supported our modest lifestyle and allowed me the opportunity to turn down this job offer. This decision of support may have been difficult for her, but to me it showed me that she trusted me and was going to be supportive of my pursuit of my dreams, our dreams.

It was a 9 to 5, set salary, and no commission. The pay wasn't bad, and as I said, I was grateful for the offer. It was a good job, but it would have gotten in the way of what I wanted, and I wasn't interested in wasting more time rather than building my dream.

The thing you need to understand about me is that I'd rather take a job where I'm offered $0 guaranteed, strictly commission, but know that the sky's the limit in terms of opportunity, rather than a place where my income is defined and limited.

I just can't wake up and go to work every morning knowing there is a finite amount of money that I can make that day. The property manager job would have taken up the heart of the day from 9 to 5 and prevented me from building my own real estate opportunities. I would have been capped at whatever the job paid. This is what is known as opportunity cost. What would that salary position have cost me in terms of opportunity?

Thank you, but no, thank you.

I wasn't born to live a life under financial constraints. I was seeking an opportunity to build my own real estate brokerage business, and my reward depended on my performance and success.

I am a gambler, and it was time to bet on myself!

That said, while I pursued starting and building back my brokerage business, I still needed to make money to live while I was trying to get back in the game. I chose jobs that left me enough time and flexibility to work on my dream while sustaining me financially.

The first job I took was as a driver, filling vending machines. My high school craps buddy, Joe, who owns a full-service vending company, needed someone to drive a route, filling vending machines for $500 a week. The hours were flexible, which suited my needs perfectly. Joe was and still is one of my best friends, and his father, John, was probably the third most influential male figure in my life growing up. John coached me in athletics and was always around when I spent time at their house. I respected him as a father and leader, and he had a strong influence on me over the years. I'm proud to say that he stood by me when I needed him, offering me a job at a vulnerable point in my life.

A couple of veteran drivers trained me on the job, and after about a month of riding along the route, I asked John a question: "Why are the drivers always putting the same things in the machines? Sometimes, we make a delivery, and the same items sell out weekly, but others just sit there. Why don't we replace those items with something that sells better?"

John's face lit up, and he said, "You did it! You get it! I wish every driver looked at the job from a business perspective. Most drivers just do their jobs and nothing else. They either don't get it, or they don't care."

It was a valuable lesson. No job is too small to make a difference to the larger organization. I was an economics major, and this seemed like simple supply and demand economics to me. Even though I didn't graduate, I am still able to apply a great deal of what I learned in college to any business, even something as simple as driving a vending route. I always strive for more, even if it's just $1 at a time; more is more.

At this point, I was carrying a mortgage and had significant expenses in my life with little disposable money. Joe told me I could eat from the product in the truck, but I was never much of a snacker or junk food guy. I wanted square meals, so as I got hungry, I would take $5-$10 from the cash bag daily to buy my breakfast or lunch. Don't get me wrong; I was acutely aware of the possibility that this could be perceived as stealing from my best friend, so I made sure to let them know, put the receipts in the bag daily, and gave them an option to dock it out of my pay at the end of the week. They never did, and never said anything about the receipts at the time, but it's humorous when we look back and talk about it now.

My second job in the summer of 2010 was at a local theme park in Kansas City called *Oceans of Fun*. It only opens in the spring and summer, and I had another buddy working there in a high position, so I asked him if I could pick up some bartending shifts on weekends. It didn't interfere with my driving job and brought in damn good tip money, up to $500 a weekend, so it was the perfect side gig. Finally, my dad and brother-in-law were working at UPS and got me a line sorting gig at the airport, Monday-Friday, 7 pm to 10 pm. I'd work at UPS 15 hours or so a week because it came with full health, dental, and vision insurance, and honestly, the pay wasn't terrible either.

These jobs didn't pay top dollar, but they afforded me the freedom to seek a position in the real estate brokerage world during the hours necessary to stake my claim in that industry. I wasn't just sitting around all day, waiting for this golden opportunity or proverbial bag of money to fall out of the sky and into my lap. I was out there hustling and busting my ass, arguably working harder than I ever have, working three jobs to make sure I was able to help my wife pay the bills and keep us afloat while keeping my ear to the ground for opportunities in the commercial real estate brokerage world.

I went from thinking that I was going to walk out of prison and into a job that would allow me to reach the goals I had set for myself while working 40-50 hours a week, to working over 80 hours a week and making much slower progress toward achieving my goals. Life threw a curveball at me, which I hadn't expected. You never know what you're going to get. Today, you may be living in the lap of luxury or scrounging around on the streets for something to eat. Tomorrow, the roles might be reversed. It's what you do with that curveball that defines your at-bat.

In July 2010, a friend and business associate who had a family brokerage company got in touch with me and said I was welcome to hang my license at his firm, Victor Ross & Co. Commercial Real Estate. This happened while I was still committed to the other jobs to keep my head above water. The commercial real estate world operates as an 8-5 Monday through Friday. I had also committed to John and Joe that I would run their route through the summer, regardless of what came about; they gave me an opportunity with flexibility, and I wasn't about to leave them high and dry. I'd run the vending route early in the morning from 5:00 am to midday for $500 a week. Then, I'd cold-call real estate prospects from noon until about 5:30 pm in the evening, go home, eat dinner, go to UPS, and work there from 7:00 pm until 10:00 pm. When I got off work, I would come home, shower, and go to bed, just to get up the following day and do it all over again. Then, on the weekends, I'd bartend at *Oceans of Fun*. This is what Dave Ramsey would call "gazelle intense," and I knew that this lifestyle was not sustainable.

I needed to generate the necessary income for my expenses, with the flexibility to dedicate time to my long-term goals. I often hear people complain that *"I don't have time,"* or *"there aren't any opportunities,"* or *"I don't have the right skills,"* or other lame excuses. I will always call bullshit on these. We all have the same twenty-four hours in the day; it's what you do with that time that defines you. There's always something you can do, especially with so many twenty-four-hour operations or online opportunities that have taken over the global market.

You don't have any computer skills? How about mowing lawns, washing cars, or flipping burgers? There are no bad jobs or jobs that are beneath you. There are only means to an end, which can take many forms.

Do whatever you need to do to survive while carving out additional time and energy toward accomplishing your long-term goals. It's all about taking control and making it happen. It's the activity that produces the result. If you're unwilling to put in the effort and do what it takes to succeed, you have nothing and no one else to blame but yourself. Too often, people play the *poor me* card and point their fingers elsewhere. The only person you should point to is the person looking back at you in the mirror.

There's no shame in hard work, multiple jobs, or manual labor. Here I was, a 28-year-old kid who'd been in the top five percent of earners as a 26-year-old kid but also been to prison and ostracized by his mentor. I could have held out and been entitled, but in reality, I felt no shame in doing any of the jobs I was doing at the time to survive and get ahead. I had to pay my dues and was happy to do so.

I did a few real estate deals with a guy I met in prison named Bob. He was in for a white-collar crime and was released around the same time I was. He had a couple of warehouse buildings available for lease in Lee's

Summit, MO, which I signed up on exclusive listings and then procured tenants for the vacancies, bringing me in almost $20,000 per deal.

I was back!

You never know from where your next opportunity might come. Everyone we meet in life enters our path for a reason, and investing time in relationship management is one of the most valuable things we can do, not just for transactional purposes, but to build meaningful, value-driven connections that deepen over time.

The brokerage business was great, don't get me wrong. I could make a lot of money brokering transactions, but to get to where I wanted to be in life, I needed to get off the transaction treadmill. I needed to use my talents and abilities to transact a massive number of high-volume deals to create income to transition to wealth.

I had to put my money to work to earn passive income through investments that make money without me needing to do any active work. I wanted to use every minute of every day doing one of these five things: prospecting, negotiating, transacting, closing, and maintaining relationships to fund and invest in real, tangible assets. Making money is one thing, but utilizing that revenue to reinvest into building a real estate and business portfolio to earn passive income in the future is how I planned to accelerate wealth accumulation with velocity.

Warren Buffett, a man with a net worth of over $130 BILLION, famously said: "If you don't find a way to make money while you sleep, you'll work until the day you die."

I don't know about you, but I'm not planning on having to work the way I used to until the day I die. I had a vision for my life and the goals I set for myself along the way.

It was time to execute.

I can walk into a dilapidated building that looks like a financial loss waiting to happen and immediately see potential where others don't. Because of my growth mindset and analytical mind, I can evaluate deals instantaneously and know whether a project is worth the risk or at what price it is worth the risk. I knew I wanted to own real estate and start other future businesses, which led me to my first real estate purchase in 2011: a 2,400 sq.ft., former veterinary clinic. It had been abandoned since 2005, trashed, stripped of copper, the roof was falling in, and it reeked of dog urine. I picked it up for $80,000 and invested another $30,000 to fix it up. Shortly after the improvements were completed, I leased the building for $1,500 a month, Triple Net Lease (NNN), meaning the tenant covered real estate taxes, building insurance, and maintenance, in addition to the base rent.

I borrowed all $110,000 for this investment from a family friend. After I paid the monthly debt service, I generated $800 in monthly positive cash flow, which allowed me to invest in additional properties while still covering the debt. It's how you accelerate asset accumulation: use primary income to generate passive income and then use that passive income to cover future acquisitions. That first property, located at 3408 Independence Ave., was the beginning of my real estate journey.

My knowledge, experience, and work ethic meant that I didn't need "help" on the business side of things. What I *needed* was a platform that would allow me to build up to where I wanted to be. Unfortunately, my relentless pursuit of financial growth hurt my relationship with my current brokerage office. I had brought in the equivalent of around 30 listings in 45 days for them. I was already closing deals. Once I retired from the vending route, I consistently came into the office first and was always the last to leave. Eventually, I realized the normal 50/50 brokerage commission-agent split wasn't enough for me. I started looking for other platforms to grow my business, with more money coming to the broker farming and hunting the land, and less to the house that sits on it.

Six months into my tenure at Victor Ross, I told my friend, Vic, I had been offered work at a different company. The new opportunity offered me the chance to be the broker, to build a team underneath me, and a 70/30 split with me being the big bite and a cap of $21,000 annually to the brokerage house on what I'd have to pay on the deals that I brought in and closed. At Victor Ross, I was paying a 50% split and no cap. I had paid as much as $50,000 in commission to the brokerage in just six short months.

This new opportunity was obviously a far better deal for me going forward. It wouldn't make sense for me to stay where I was. It was a decision that was going to benefit me and my family, not the brokerage. Still, the decision temporarily strained our friendship, as he was hurt that I was leaving after he had given me a chance.

I moved to Keller Williams Commercial (KW Commercial) from Victor Ross in January 2011. KW Commercial had just launched its commercial platform a short time prior to my joining. They had recruited Buddy Norman, a well-respected commercial broker from the Staubach Company out of Texas, to head up the commercial division. He was not only bringing structure, access to real estate forms and documents, training, and a platform to grow, but also potential national clients and tenant representation deals from which I could benefit greatly.

In addition, there was a tremendous referral network from their residential agent platform. Keller Williams had and still has a massive residential real estate platform, with nearly 190,000 agents, all of whom I saw as a potential referring source. This was the kind of company where I could see myself living up to my potential.

Through this transition, I still bartended on weekends through 2011 and continued my night job at UPS. I worked at UPS for 7 years, through 2017. So, even though I had my broker's license and was back to making well over six figures a year as a broker, I still did these other jobs because I knew I wasn't where I needed or wanted to be, and I wanted to accelerate my vision. Plus, working at UPS came with the medical insurance I mentioned earlier, and that was quite a cost savings to a 1099 Misc. who had a wife in her childbearing years and the desire to grow our family.

Commercial real estate and residential real estate are two very different businesses. The commercial real estate business is all about numbers, analytics, knowledge, and having the confidence to know how to talk to a client and which levers to pull in the negotiation. I'm an expert in this case. No one knows more than I do, is better at numbers, and has more confidence (perceptually). This is my vocation and my passion. I have a mind for analytics, sales, and business in general. Not only do I know the market, but I also know how to speak to clients in a way that is relatable to them and benefits them. Putting their pocketbook ahead of mine led to better relationships, continued repeat customers, and greater percentages of deals being closed. The knowledge and learning curve for a commercial real estate agent is significantly longer than for a residential one, which is why these agents were low-hanging fruit for me to build my business.

I would go to the weekly residential agent meetings in Kansas City and ask for a few minutes from the team leader to address the other agents. Then, I'd ask them questions about certain types of leases or due diligence items that a real estate agent should know to adequately and best serve their client in commercial transactions. I would explain to them the knowledge and abilities I have as a commercial closer, and that these skills have been taught and polished through years of practice and success. These agents didn't have access to commercial contractual documents, CoStar, or Loopnet, which offer commercial listing services, comparable sale analysis, market data, and marketing platforms. These services are way too expensive for a one-off residential agent to cover the costs.

I would further explain to them that there are no seller disclosures in the commercial world. One slip-up, misrepresentation, false promise, or lack of knowledge, and these residential agents could expose their clients or themselves to substantial liability. It was easier, and there was a higher likelihood that I would close their client or prospect than they would. I would pay them 25% of the commission for doing nothing but making a connection if/when it closed. Sometimes, I'd walk out of those meetings with 7 or 8 referrals, and while they weren't all home runs, many of those referrals converted to listings or representation agreements, where I would exclusively represent the buyer/tenant or seller/landlord. One of those referrals converted into a $4 million transaction. The split on that deal earned the referring agent $30,000. That's $30,000 they probably wouldn't have had if I hadn't prospected that deal.

After my first full year at KW Commercial, I was one of the top five agents in the country and was awarded the opportunity to sit on the top broker panel at the National Convention in Austin, Texas. I sat on a panel of experts and talked to other agents, conveying my experience and expertise. I desired to use the KW platform to accelerate the growth of my business. As I continued to grow my business under this platform, I couldn't service my client base by myself; I needed a team. This was a great way of building a book of businesses and a team of agents who could help me break out on my own and start my own company. I wanted to be the guy who received part of the commission splits from my agents, not the one paying them.

Chapter 3:
Mindset

"Whether you believe you can,
or believe you can't, you're right." —Henry Ford

I've talked a lot so far about *what* I did during my time in prison and the first few years after my release, but I haven't really explained how it was possible. I was told by more than a few people that prison would ruin my life and everything I had worked to build. Fortunately, their opinions went in one ear and out the other. The fact that I'm strong-willed should be obvious by now, but turning life's obstacles into opportunities for growth and development takes more than just willpower; it takes the right mindset.

There's a lot to be said on the subject of mindset. I highly recommend reading the book by Dr. Carol Dweck, an American psychologist who studies mindset and motivation. This book helped me put into words the way I see the world.

Have you ever wondered why some people seem able to thrive, regardless of their personal circumstances, while others always seem to find excuses for their poor performance? Mindset has a lot to do with it.

Think about the following questions:

- Do you believe that your intelligence is set in stone, or do you think that you can continue to learn and grow as you age?
- Do you pursue interests, such as picking up a new hobby, even if you think it might be difficult to learn or you might not be very good at it, or do you stick to what you know because you're afraid of failing at something new?

- Do you think that talent is more important than effort when it comes to academics, athletics, music, or art, or do you believe that hard work counts just as much or more?
- Do you often feel that things outside your control hold you back from achieving your goals, or do you see obstacles as opportunities?
- Do you look for reasons to explain away someone else's success, or do you appreciate the hard work that went into their accomplishments?

How you answer these questions reveals a lot about your mindset.

Mindset, at its simplest, is the way you see the world and your place in it.

People with a fixed mindset believe that many things are mostly beyond our control and are fixed from the outset. They often see themselves and others as fitting into rigid, unalterable categories.

People are either smart or not. Athletic or not. Talented or not.

They tend to believe that we are born with certain traits that give a person advantages or disadvantages in life. More importantly, they place less emphasis on effort and hard work in developing certain traits and abilities than they do on what they deem to be natural talents and abilities. You've either got it or you don't.

As a result, many people with a fixed mindset become strongly attached to the identities they've adopted that are tied to their perceived talents or skills. The problem is that these identities often change over time. This is true for both positive and negative identities.

The kid who is always picked last for pick-up basketball may believe they are just not athletic. They might grow up avoiding sports, believing they will never be good at physical activity. This can lead to missing out on pursuing any physical or sports-related interests later in life.

Even so-called positive labels can lead to anxiety and limiting beliefs. The gifted child might take pride in that identity for a time, but what happens when they encounter a subject they find difficult? Or when another child surpasses their academic achievements, causing them to question their actual intelligence? They may wonder, *Am I not that smart after all?*

If a child (or an adult) has a fixed mindset, they may find any level of failure to be overwhelming and further proof that they aren't as smart as they were led to believe. Some people would rather not try than try and fail, as failure is tied to their self-worth. I'll talk more about failure later in the chapter, but how I view failure is a huge factor in my success.

A fixed mindset can extend beyond personal traits to how someone views their circumstances. At the same time, it's true that some people are given a head start in life, but deciding that you've lost the game before you even start is a limiting belief characteristic of a fixed mindset. Fixed mindsets lead to excuses, a lack of effort, and a belief that life controls you rather than seeing life as a wealth of opportunity. Your mindset colors your view on life.

Having a growth mindset is the exact opposite. It is the belief in limitless potential. The idea that no matter where you find yourself, that is only the starting point for future growth and improvement through effort. When I got out of prison, more than a few people doubted my ability to bounce back and be successful. Thankfully, I wasn't one of them! My mindset was focused on continuous improvement. I viewed challenges as opportunities, took responsibility for my actions, and looked for solutions to unexpected obstacles. Instead of spending my days looking to lay blame elsewhere, I took ownership of my failures and successes.

This isn't about toxic positivity or being delusional about who we are and where we are in life. Pretending that everything is fine when it's not is not a characteristic of a growth mindset. Those tend to be characteristics of a fixed mindset, where self-worth is tied to arbitrary, innate characteristics or random life circumstances. If your success depends on something outside your control, it's in your best interests to turn a blind eye when something goes wrong.

Those with a growth mindset are often better able to evaluate their abilities accurately and don't feel the need to exaggerate or misrepresent their skills. They believe that they can improve over time with hard work and dedication. They exhibit grit, passion, perseverance, determination, and resilience —all of which are essential leadership qualities.

One way to accelerate your growth mindset is by putting the four Cs into practice.

Control: This is less about controlling what happens than controlling your reactions to things. Learning to channel our emotions constructively is key to controlling our responses to challenges. I learned a lot about emotional control during my time in prison, and it has served me well ever since.

Commitment: People with a growth mindset can better manage frustration and show greater resilience in the face of challenges. This shows up as dedication and perseverance to achieve goals, even through difficulties. My goal of financial success was challenged almost immediately upon my release. Rather than giving up, I doubled down on my commitment to achieve the success I dreamed about.

Challenge: Viewing obstacles as opportunities for growth with a positive outlook. Every challenge is a chance to learn something, not a reason to quit. The belief that you can do hard things is worth more than most people realize.

Confidence: Believing in your ability to handle challenges and improve over time is not arrogant—it is a necessary condition for success. True confidence doesn't mean that you think you know everything, but rather that you trust in your ability to figure it out or to get the help you need to improve your chances of success.

Failure is a key component of any success story. Nobody likes to fail, but we all do at one point or another. The key isn't whether you fail; it's how you handle failure when it happens. For me, failure is an opportunity to grow. You may have heard the saying, *Fail. Fail again. Fail better.* This philosophy sums up a growth mindset's approach to failure. Failure is a steppingstone to bigger and better things.

Once you get over the fear of failure, you're free.

Failure leads to freedom. Freedom to try again. Freedom to aim higher, bigger, better. This will lead to a life of abundance.

Your mindset is a massive determining factor in just how far you'll go in life and how much you'll achieve both in business and in your personal life. Once you separate your self-worth from whether or not you succeed at everything you try, you will be willing to try so many more things.

Which mindset do you hold?

For me, there are no limits. I don't like imposing any restraints on myself. I want to have the freedom to achieve as much as I possibly can by learning as much as I possibly can.

This principle of embracing the growth mindset can be applied universally. Mindset influences everything a person thinks and does. The benefits of a growth mindset in your personal life, your interpersonal relationships, and personal well-being are undeniable. Individuals with a growth mindset prioritize self-improvement, seek partners and friends who inspire them to learn and grow, value diverse perspectives, and enjoy surrounding themselves with people who challenge their thinking.

They are less concerned with being the most knowledgeable in the room and more focused on expanding their horizons. A growth mindset encourages the ability to adapt, learn, and grow — not only in facing challenges in external relationships but also in navigating the complexities of the relationship you have with yourself and your self-growth.

In the world of business, a growth mindset promotes resilience and innovation, invaluable assets in this ever-evolving realm. A leader who encourages a growth mindset within their company empowers their teams to pursue innovation and excellence, challenging them to embrace any failures and challenges that may cross their paths. As an entrepreneur, it was this mindset that allowed me to trust my instincts and take calculated risks to help me build my business.

By the end of 2015, just five years after my release from prison, I started my own commercial real estate brokerage company. I named it "Opes," which is the short/plural form of opulent, which means abundance, resources, and wealth. Within a few years, I had gone from prisoner to being outcast by my uncle, to blue-collar multi-job worker hustling my ass off, to realtor with KW and then finally to having my broker's license and my own business with a small established team. If you can dream it, with the right mindset, you can achieve it.

Where your attention goes, energy flows.

Rather than dwelling on the past or coming up with all the reasons why achieving my dreams was too hard, I focused on the belief that I could take those obstacles and turn them into lessons and opportunities for change. I applied the 4 Cs by taking control of my reactions to disappointments and setbacks, committing myself to my goals in every area of life, viewing challenges as opportunities, and being confident in my ability to achieve what I set out to accomplish, and even more.

To continue cultivating a growth mindset, it's crucial to discuss the significance of mindfulness and positivity regarding our daily thoughts. The thoughts we nurture, and our mental habits have profound implications on our personal and professional lives. During the months I spent in prison, giving in to thoughts of defeat and disappointment would have been the easy choice. There was enough of it to go around, and as we all know, misery loves company.

When all you see around you is failure and disappointment, allowing your thoughts to run rampant and focusing only on the negative takes very little effort, if any. Mindfulness—the awareness of your thought patterns—can propel you toward success or anchor you in a pit of despair.

Every single day, we are bombarded with a horde of thoughts. On average, you think around 60,000 thoughts a day. You are probably not even consciously aware of most of them as they come and go throughout your day. Many thoughts are fleeting, like: *"It's hot outside," "There goes an airplane overhead,"* or even *"I'm hungry."* Others linger longer and can influence both your mood and consequent actions.

Your true power lies in realizing that you have a choice regarding which thoughts you focus on. People who consistently focus on negative thoughts, dwelling on setbacks, negativity, or injustices, often find themselves trapped in a cycle of pessimism and defeat. This cycle of habitual negativity can cloud your judgment, stifle your creativity, and ultimately hinder your performance both in your business and personal lives.

As a business owner and leader, I constantly have to filter through thoughts about market conditions, what's best for my businesses, which avenues we should take and which we should steer clear of, how to motivate my teams, how to be a good leader, how to be better than our competitors, etc. If I were to allow myself to only focus on the negative thoughts that pop into my head daily, I would've given up a long time ago. Choosing to only see resistance and struggle instead of the opportunities that lie beyond will cause you to miss out on being proactive, fail to find unique solutions to any problems that pop up along the way, and miss the chance for innovation and growth. This can drag down your team's morale and creativity, which are crucial elements for transformation and problem-solving in any competitive landscape.

On the flip side, being mindful of your thought patterns and intentionally focusing on positive and constructive thoughts can change the game. But there's more to it than just "thinking positive thoughts." It's about creating a mindset that promotes actively seeking opportunities, learning from setbacks, and remaining open to new ideas and solutions instead of clinging to unhelpful or outdated ways of doing things. The world is forever changing at a rapid rate, and you need to be open to changing with it; otherwise, you'll get left behind. I'm not saying that you should simply ignore the potential challenges and risks you may face. What I'm saying is that I've learned that it is important to approach these with a solution-oriented mindset.

Learn to see the potential opportunity when things don't go your way. Didn't get that deal you were after? Good. It allows you to go back to the drawing board and assess what you could have done differently or better. Or, perhaps it means recognizing that it might not have been the right opportunity for your purposes or goals and that there's something better out there. Choose to find the good that comes from when something goes bad. Sometimes, the best deals are the ones you don't do!

Mindfulness means being aware of your thought patterns and self-talk and consciously choosing to change them when they don't serve you.

Our brains are designed to naturally pay more attention to negative environmental influences than to positive ones. This is part of the survival mechanism that has allowed us to make it this far as a species. It's called negativity bias. The problem is that this mechanism is useful when you live in the wild and need to pay attention to all the possible threats to your survival at any given moment, like hazardous weather, poisonous plants, or dangerous animals. However, when you live in the modern world like most of us do, if you don't practice enough self-awareness to mind the thoughts you continuously pay attention to, you can get stuck in a negative feedback loop. One geared towards a mindset of scarcity.

Imagine if I had allowed myself to focus only on the challenges I have faced in my life, or taken a limited-opportunity job that was available to me, and maintained complacency. I would not even own my own business, let alone multiple businesses.

I wouldn't have the lifestyle and large family that I enjoy now.

No one can afford not to have a positive growth mindset that seeks opportunity and learns from setbacks. Don't allow distractions to pull you off course or allow negative thoughts to invade and alter your mindset. It's not worth it, and I don't have time for it. Neither do you.

Being mindful of your thoughts and deliberately guiding them toward growth and learning can cultivate a mindset equipped for success. Gently steer your thoughts toward positivity, possibility, and productivity. The quality of your thoughts ultimately dictates the quality of your life, making it essential to foster a disciplined inner landscape that aligns with your aspirations and values.

A helpful tool for becoming more aware of your daily thoughts and thought processes is a thought diary. Do this for a month: every day, keep a diary of your thoughts. You won't be able to note down all 60,000. Focus on keeping track of your negative thoughts. Whenever you become aware of a negative thought or catch yourself dwelling on the negative, write it down. Also, write down what might have prompted that thought.

What was going on around and inside of you at the time?

What emotion did the thought invoke?

Making yourself more aware of your thoughts is not only helpful in fostering more positive thoughts and thought processes but also helps to identify areas of your life where change is needed. Instead of allowing yourself to remain in an environment that is not conducive to growth or complaining without taking action, you can then assess the situation from a more objective standpoint and make the necessary changes, like finding a new job or starting your own business on the side until you can exit your current negative situation.

When you become more aware of your thoughts, you may find that the negative outweighs the positive. Negative self-belief and negative self-talk may seem inconsequential, but they have a huge impact on your mindset, outlook, and results. Using the journal to help reframe your thoughts is a great first step. The next step is to become aware of how those thoughts express themselves out loud.

Complaining! Did you hear that?

Complaining may seem pretty harmless as a venting mechanism and everyday outlet for frustrations of daily life, but when it comes to building healthy habits, complaining works against you, insidiously infiltrating all your hard work and undoing it.

To me, there is nothing more draining than habitual complainers. Especially those who always complain but never do anything to change their situation. The pessimists and energy vampires. I steer clear of them as far as possible. It's not only counter-productive; it can also have a significantly negative impact on your mental health and overall quality of life.

When you complain regularly, the neurons in your brain organize themselves to strengthen this habit. Your brain doesn't know the difference between positive and negative. It just organizes itself according to what you allow yourself to focus on. The more you complain, the stronger those connections become, and the more you can spot anything remotely negative in your environment. Then, it becomes a cycle. The more it feeds your habit of complaining, the sicker, darker, and more stifled your world becomes, and unbeknownst to you, there is additional collateral damage done.

A seemingly innocuous habit can set a tone of negativity that extends beyond momentary grievances. It can affect your outlook on life, relationships, health, and even professional success. It shifts your focus away from problem-solving and towards problem-dwelling, leading you down a rabbit hole of frustration and despair.

There have been people in my life whom I've had to let go of because of their constant complaining. I just cannot stomach the effect it has on me. It really does feel like the energy is being sucked right out of me, leaving me feeling utterly depleted. While we all need an empathetic ear sometimes, constant negativity can be draining and alienate your friends, family, and colleagues. Over time, this can lead you to lose important people and connections in your life. People are naturally drawn to others who uplift them, and may begin to distance themselves from you if you constantly contribute a negative vibe to your interactions.

In a professional context, people who chronically complain are often seen as less effective and less desirable as employees. Unless it's someone willing to work on themselves and do something to change their situation, I've found chronic complainers to be less capable of handling adversity, less creative, less likely to take proactive steps toward change, and more likely to drag the people around them down with them. If you're a chronic complainer, it limits your opportunities, especially for leadership roles and professional growth, as the ability to manage challenges constructively is a key trait of any successful professional. Chronic complainers tend to poison the well and are adept at seeking more negativity.

They have a problem for every solution.

Balancing your perspective is crucial to ensure that complaining doesn't become your predominant mode of expression. Cultivating an *attitude of gratitude*, focusing on solutions, and maintaining a constructive outlook can minimize the desire to complain and enhance your overall life satisfaction and effectiveness in handling the challenges you will undoubtedly face.

Another type of person to avoid is someone who loves to gossip. Gossip is the Devil's radio. Fire and weapons are slow engines of destruction compared to the tongue of a Gossip. People who like to gossip do so to compensate for their low self-esteem. They don't want to do anything about their situation, so they use gossip to either seek attention or deflect it. It is never driven by positivity or kindness; it is only driven by pride and the burning desire to feel better and more important than others.

These people usually love creating drama and conflict to satisfy their own insecurities. They find temporary relief from the pain of their low self-esteem and inner conflict by judging others. Only small-minded people with a fixed mindset will ever entertain gossip. So, I would advise you to steer clear of those around the water cooler and coffee pot, unless they're discussing ideas, strategies, and goals, whether in business or life in general.

The older I get, the more I realize that what I really want is peace. Peace of mind and peace of heart. My focus has become more and more about doing right by myself and the people who love and care for and about me. The more time passes and the busier I become, the less drama I can handle in my life. When we're younger, we have more capacity for putting up with all kinds of distractions: the envy, the jealousy, the haters who feel that the only way to elevate themselves is by putting down others.

I'd say that once you hit your forties, your tolerance level decreases by a significant margin with each passing year. With age and wisdom comes the realization that what others think of you is none of your business and that you don't need to do anything to validate your actions or explain yourself to anyone. I don't have time for people who are rude, unnecessarily disrespectful, out to hurt, or are inconsiderate of others.

Find what brings you peace, and focus on doing more of that!

For me, it's spending time with family and friends—those who love me unconditionally and genuinely for who I am, whether we're playing golf, swimming, vacationing, or just hanging out.

It's about mentoring and guiding kids on the baseball field, teaching them valuable lessons that I've learned along the way, and developing them both inside and outside the lines. Knowing that I am developing leaders within my companies, empowering and elevating these leaders within our organizations to succeed in my absence, and providing me with more flexibility and peace of mind.

Giving back to the community, doing philanthropic work, and knowing that my talents and abilities don't just selfishly help me and my family, but also help those around me. I thank God daily for the talents and abilities I was given and the life that He afforded me, as well as for my wonderful wife and four beautiful children. We have our health, family, friends, and the mindset that is always willing. I'm never finished; I'm always looking to grow and improve, and that gives me the deepest peace. If you're not growing, you're dying. Just like I tell my kids, get better every day!

It's equally crucial to emphasize the importance of emotional regulation in cultivating a resilient and positive growth mindset. The ability to manage and regulate your emotions is not just a personal asset; it's a fundamental skill that impacts every aspect of your life, from personal relationships to professional success. Sadly, it's a skill that very few people are ever taught, and unless you make a point of teaching yourself how to regulate your own emotions, I'm afraid you may never acquire it.

Emotional regulation involves understanding, processing, and effectively managing one's emotional responses in various situations. It enables one to face challenges and setbacks with a clear mind and a balanced perspective. This skill is particularly vital in high-stress environments such as the workplace, where emotional reactivity can cloud judgment, impair decision-making, and lead to unnecessary conflict. It is equally important in our personal relationships.

If you cannot regulate your emotions and constantly lose your cool and attack those around you, are abrupt, or take your frustrations out on the people you care about, such actions tear apart and weaken those relationships. When you learn to control your emotions and communicate with them rather than bottling them up to the point of explosion, you can communicate more effectively, build stronger bonds, and navigate personal challenges with greater ease. By understanding and managing your emotions, you can avoid having your emotions control your behavior in ways that could damage important relationships and instead respond in ways that encourage mutual respect and understanding.

The ability to regulate your own emotions also contributes to a more adaptive and proactive approach to problem-solving. All of life is navigating and solving a series of problems. When you manage your emotional responses, you are better equipped to assess situations objectively, identify potential solutions, and take decisive action without being overwhelmed by negative emotions. Emotions are inevitable; however, it doesn't mean that you should allow them to rule your life. To allow yourself to make the best decisions in every area of life, you need to foster the ability to put your emotions aside to focus on the problem at hand in a more rational and practical manner.

Perhaps most importantly, developing emotional regulation helps us maintain our mental health. The same goes for steering clear of complaining and gossiping, of course. Practicing emotional regulation techniques can help reduce the likelihood of experiencing extreme stress, anxiety, and depression, conditions that all have the potential to significantly negatively impact one's life.

When I coach kids' baseball, it's not the kids who have the hardest time controlling their emotions; it's the parents. Sometimes, their anger or frustration is aimed at the umps; sometimes, it's at the parents of the other team or even at their own kids. And sometimes, it's directed at me. They wanted their child placed in a different position, to have a better at bat, or to somehow receive preferential treatment. While many parents approach these situations calmly, there are always those who lose their cool and act worse than the kids.

So, I help all parents manage their emotions by having them sign a contract at the beginning of the season, stipulating that any complaints must be held for 24 hours following a game before being heard by me. This gives everyone a chance to cool off before discussing topics that evoke strong emotions. Arguing in the heat of the moment never solves anything, and 9 times out of 10, the parent realizes that what they were so angry about the day before isn't even worth discussing with me.

This technique also sets a great example for the kids. No child wants to be caught between their parents and their coach or see their parents fly off the handle in public. Having an example to draw from in their own lives gives them a framework for dealing with anger.

Like all other habits, mastering the art of regulating your own emotions takes regular practice. Integrating tools and techniques like deep breathing exercises or mindfulness meditation into your daily routine can help strengthen your ability to self-regulate and improve your emotional resilience.

I'm not an expert, but I do certain things that help me keep cool in stressful situations.

I'd like to refer back to the thought diary exercise. In addition to keeping track of your negative thoughts, I suggest you note the accompanying emotions. I love this exercise because it's like killing two birds with one stone. Becoming more aware of the emotions that accompany your thought processes will help you better identify the reasons behind them. We don't just experience emotions for no reason. There's always a stimulus involved. When you can identify that stimulus and teach yourself how to pause reacting on impulse, you can better regulate your thoughts, emotions, and behaviors.

Much like the 24-hour contract I use when coaching, I make a point to try never to have a knee-jerk response. I pause and let some time pass before responding to something that has upset or annoyed me. At work, I may take a walk around the building and think about the ramifications of three different responses before I choose one that will have the best outcome. I may even type out an email response, only to save it and return to it an hour later, once I've cooled down, to see if the response is justified.

At home, this may mean taking a break before getting into an unnecessary argument or telling your kids you need a few minutes before having a conversation about something they did that upset you. It's realizing that while something out of your control may trigger an emotion, how you manage that emotion and react outwardly is completely within your control. Furthermore, how you react will affect the outcome of the issue at hand.

Embracing both mindful thinking and emotional regulation creates this powerful synergy that can dramatically increase your effectiveness in all areas of your life. This dual approach ensures that you not only think optimally but also feel optimally, enabling you to perform at your best under any circumstances. One of the best gifts you can give yourself in life is to accept the fact that you, and only you, are responsible for the thoughts you focus on and the consequent emotions and behaviors.

Chapter 4:
Your Values Inform Your Goals

"Your beliefs become your thoughts, your thoughts become your words, your words become your actions, your actions become your habits, your habits become your values, your values become your destiny."
—Mahatma Gandhi

Our world, as we perceive it, is reduced to those items on which we choose to focus. So, if you choose to focus on how few resources and opportunities are available to you, that's all you'll ever see and have. But if you choose to focus on possibilities, growth, and what *is* available, your world begins to expand in those directions. And the kicker is—either one is within your control.

I often see people pursuing big goals that have nothing in common with their values in life. Something I've learned along the way is that life isn't, or shouldn't be, all about who has the fanciest car or who has the largest, most expensive mansion. They say, *Money can't buy you happiness.* However, I believe it can, if what you do with your money is in alignment with your values in life.

Do you know what your values are? Have you ever taken the time to step back and figure out what you value most in life? Is it family, faith, good health, friendship, or honesty?

Your values become your destiny because they are your compass in life. If you value good health, you're probably hitting the gym at least a few times a week or engaging in some form of physical activity regularly. You're probably someone who minds what you eat and goes for regular checkups. If you don't value good health, you probably do the opposite. If you value honesty and work ethic, you probably pride yourself on the quality of your work and value relationships. Of course, these are just a few examples, but if you want to live a life of fulfillment, believe me when I say your conduct needs to be aligned with your values.

I know what my values are in life.

I value my family and spending time with my wife and kids, so I try to avoid working on weekends. I value being an exemplary leader to others and pride myself on leading by example. I value honesty, which is why I've always been open and upfront about my past. I value commitment, integrity and effort, so I always put 100% into whatever I do. I value freedom, so my goal has always been to make so much money while I sleep that I can use my time doing things I'm passionate about other than working. I value my faith, which, to me, is a strong belief in God. I know I will never be perfect; there is one God, and I'm not Him, so I must attend church weekly, confess my sins, and pray for strength and guidance to better myself. This is key to my growing in every aspect of life, as belief in someone greater than yourself minimizes ego.

I asked my wife to share her thoughts on how my family values are reflected in my actions as a husband and father. Here's what she had to say:

"I have been married to Chuck for 14 years and together for 20. He has inspired me to be the person I am today. We chose each other and put one another first over anything. His striving to get what he wants and accomplish his goals is unbelievable. He always achieves it. If he says he's going to do something, he does it. But the best part of him is watching him be a father. To say he is a good dad is an understatement. The way he doesn't miss anything. Whether it be sporting events, school programs, dances, playing

outside, movie nights, birthday celebrations, or date nights, he doesn't miss any of it. He juggles all this and runs many, many businesses. He is our Superman. I couldn't have chosen a better person. Our kids and I are so lucky to have him."
—Annamarie Cuda

You have to figure out what you value in life first, then align your goals with those values before you start wasting time on avenues that lead nowhere, or worse, to places like Leavenworth Corrections Corporation of America. If possible, learn from others' mistakes so you don't waste time making the same ones. If you do have to learn from your own mistakes, fail fast.

If you've never taken the time to formally identify your values, I urge you to do so now.

First, list the people and things in life that are most important to you, and then organize them into categories. These become your personal values. For example, my wife and kids, along with extended family members, all fall under family. Friends and acquaintances may be a different category. Health, wealth, travel...don't limit yourself when making the list. Eventually, you will begin narrowing it down to the values most important to you. Some people prioritize their values in hierarchical order, while others don't. How you organize them is up to you.

If you're unsure what your values are or what values exist, look at the list of common personal values below. Which of the values on this list do you feel most drawn to?

Authenticity	Family	Poise
Achievement	Friendship	Popularity
Adventure	Fun	Recognition
Authority	Growth	Religion
Autonomy	Happiness	Reputation
Balance	Honesty	Respect
Beauty	Integrity	Responsibility
Boldness	Influence	Security
Compassion	Justice	Self-Respect
Challenge	Kindness	Service
Citizenship	Knowledge	Spirituality
Community	Leadership	Stability
Competency	Learning	Success
Contribution	Love	Status
Creativity	Loyalty	Tradition
Curiosity	Meaningful Work	Trust
Determination	Openness	Usefulness
Fairness	Optimism	Unity
Faith	Peace	Wealth
Fame	Pleasure	Wisdom

You will discover or determine your values by looking at the list and identifying the words associated with things that are important to you and bring you happiness, fulfillment, and gratification. Next, to live a life by design congruent with the values you've identified, you need to set goals that align with your values, making you more likely to achieve them. I know that something I value but haven't been prioritizing lately in my life is my health. Since I run so many businesses, am involved in various philanthropic projects, and have a busy family life, I often end up eating unhealthy, ultra-processed takeout food instead of a healthier option.

The upside to this realization is that I now know what needs changing in that area of my life. I just need to treat it like I do my businesses and put the systems in place to ensure I eat healthy, nutritious food. It's not my wife's, kids', or anybody else's fault. I ultimately make my own decisions, so it's all on me.

Review your list, and think about how you spend your time. Is it an accurate reflection of what's important to you?

I'm a practical guy. I have responsibilities and commitments, but I try to ensure that as many of them as possible serve my values. Money, for me, is a means to an end. It allows me the freedom to spend time with my family and friends and invest in projects I care about. Work provides a level of personal and professional satisfaction, but I'm careful to make sure that it doesn't consume my life. There are things I value more than money. Raising money to help those in need is one of them. This quote from Denise Wiese, Director of Light the Night, Leukemia and Lymphoma Society (LLS), sums up her perception of me.

"Simply put, Chuck genuinely cares. What has stuck with me and I admire most about Chuck is his ability just simply to go for it. Whether in business or philanthropy, he does not hesitate to move the needle. I'm sure Chuck has heard "no" or "that isn't possible" many times. But that has not slowed him down or weighed on him as he continued to make the asks. Chuck is also a leader in balancing a very hectic work-life balance. He has let me know that his family will always come first. I am sure this is not an easy task, and he weighs this carefully before making any decision in business and his volunteer work."

The next step in pursuing your identified values is to determine how you live your life and whether you are in alignment with your stated values. We need to check that our conduct pursues the fulfillment of our values.

There's no point climbing to the top of the ladder if it's leaning against the wrong wall.

Spend a week keeping track of how you spend your time. Be ruthless. How many hours a day do you spend working, with family, exercising? How many hours a week do you spend scrolling on your phone? Watching TV? At the end of the week, take stock and be honest with yourself. If a stranger were to conclude your values based on how you spend your days, would they get it right? Put your time where your heart is.

Then, devise a plan to shift your time to align with your values. Make sure you're realistic, and understand that you may not be able to change everything all at once. Start with the non-negotiable commitments. Family may be more important to you than work, but you may need work to sustain a lifestyle that allows you to spend more time with your family. If your work takes up more time than you would like, perhaps it's time to make a plan to change that over the next six months.

Next, rearrange your free time to better align with your values. If lifelong learning is a value, replace 30 minutes of social media a day with reading, an online course, or a new hobby. You get the picture.

The key to real productivity is designing your day around what actually works for you, not what someone else swears by. If hitting the gym at 6:00 a.m. leaves you dragging through the rest of the day, then maybe that's not your optimal time. It's not about following rigid routines just because they're popular; it's about aligning your schedule with your energy, focus, and goals. When you build your day with intention, every activity—from workouts to work projects—has a better chance of being effective. The goal isn't just to stay busy; it's to move with purpose and maximize your potential across the board.

Without this direction, you will wander aimlessly through life, like a ship without a captain. You first need to know where you are going. Then, you need to know how you are going to get there. The best way to do this is to identify your values, create goals for living them, and then break those goals into measurable, manageable chunks called milestones. One powerful tool that helps bring those values and goals to life is a vision board.

I am a strong believer in using vision boards. They can be created manually, on a large poster board, or online using an app or program that allows you to add visuals. A vision board is a visual manifestation of your dreams and goals for the future. It allows you to see the life you want to make a reality at a single glance. It can incorporate real photos, doodles, or other images that clearly show your vision for your life.

Just to give you an idea, my vision at the beginning of 2012 included the following:

- A photo of a father and son playing baseball
- A photo of a family at Disney World with Mickey Mouse
- A cover of Forbes magazine, as it was a goal or dream of mine to be in the Forbes Billionaire edition

- The list of top 25 commercial brokerage companies in KC by way of volume from Ingram's magazine book of lists - I needed to make this list
- A picture of a guy ringing the NYSE stock exchange bell after taking a company public
- Men in nice, high-dollar suits, obviously executive-level status, Rolex watches, nice shoes, and accessories
- A picture of a Lamborghini and another of a private jet
- Pictures of beaches, luxury islands, vacation homes, and mansions
- Pictures of Gordon Gekko from the movie Wall Street and commercial real estate buildings.

These are just a handful of things I set my sights on achieving.

Once you have a vision, you need a plan to achieve it. Learning to set strong goals and then execute them with precision is what has helped me achieve success. There are several goal-setting methods, but the one that has worked for me is the SMART goals model. If you've never heard of SMART goals, it's an acronym that stands for:

S - Specific
M - Measurable
A - Achievable
R - Relevant
T - Time-bound

For example, let's say you want to become more physically active and lose 10 pounds because your doctor has advised you to do so.

Goal: I will lose 10 pounds.

This goal alone is too vague to be effective. A SMART goal is more likely to lead to success.

A SMART goal might look like this: I will lose 10 pounds by going to the gym close to my place of work on Monday, Wednesday, and Friday mornings from 6 a.m. to 7 a.m. for the next 2 months, losing an average of 1-2 pounds per week.

Specific: The new goal lays out more details, including when, where, and how you plan to lose the weight, the average number of pounds per week needed to stay on track, and a timeframe for completion. The weekly 1-2 pound weight loss markers are *milestones* that break down the larger goals into smaller, manageable chunks.

Measurable: A goal must be measurable along the way to increase the chance of success. Weighing yourself once at the end of the two months is technically measurable, in that you will have lost the 10 pounds or not, but at that point, it's too late to course-correct. In our example, a measurable weekly milestone of 1-2 pounds a week is a better way to keep track of the weight loss over an 8-week (2-month) period. If you do not lose weight after 3 weeks, you have enough time to correct and still meet your goal.

Achievable: Many people set aspirational goals that are not necessarily achievable in the allotted time. Losing 10 pounds in 2 days might be something a boxer does to make weight for a fight, but it's not healthy or realistic for the average person. A goal that's not achievable based on the circumstances will be abandoned. That doesn't mean you shouldn't dream big. I do. It does mean that big dreams must be broken into achievable milestones to be realistic.

Relevant: Is the goal something you really want, or is it just something you feel you should want? In our example, weight loss is recommended for health-related reasons, making it relevant. It's also important not to get tied up in irrelevant details. Don't put off heading to the gym until you have new shoes. Just get started.

Time-bound: The original goal did not include a timeline for losing weight. Timelines keep you on track, though it is important to have some flexibility. Losing 10 pounds in 3 months is better than losing no weight because you realize after 1 month that you will not reach your goal by the original date.

My goals and vision of what I want to achieve in life have always been pretty audacious. I have always been a high-functioning visionary with big dreams and bigger visions and goals. I also feel that I can complete most people's 90-day plans in 30 days, whereas it would take them 270 days to complete my 90-day plan.

People ask me how I do everything that I do. It's simple. I don't watch TV. I don't have social media, I don't gossip, and I don't waste my time on activities that don't align with my values. Why aren't you doing the same? Why aren't you trying to squeeze as much life as possible into every second of every day you are given? I don't want to get to the end and regret not having taken a chance, not having given as much as I could have to my wife, kids, businesses, or employees who implement my strategy and growth, or not having spent enough time with the people who matter most to me.

For this reason, planning is a big part of how I manage to fit in everything important to me. My values determine my goals and are the blueprint for how I plan out and schedule my days, weeks, and months.

The harder I work, the luckier I get!

Luck has nothing to do with success. Many highly successful people have expressed the same sentiment because they know what "hard work" means and looks like. Luck is a result of chance rather than someone's hard work, calculation, analytics, assessment and evaluation of opportunity, risk tolerance, and ability. Perhaps people will say there's a bit of luck involved in any sphere of your life, even in becoming successful. In my experience, luck in business is perception; it is merely the point where opportunity and preparation meet. I never once heard someone say that I was unlucky when I failed in business ventures or deals.

Preparation is something that I highly value. I always ensure that I'm prepared. Success takes (1) consistent, (2) strategic, and (3) intentional effort.

Effort must be **consistent** because it's not the big, showy actions that get the biggest results, but the small, daily ones that add up to big changes over time. Consistency means showing up even when you don't want to. Too many people rely on motivation, only to struggle when it runs out. Motivation is great for getting you started, but it wanes over time. We don't always have the motivation to do the things we know we should. That's where consistency steps in. You exercise three days a week because you are committed to being consistent, not because you always feel like it. Those consistent sessions add up to big results.

Effort must be **strategic** because if you're putting effort into things that take up time and those efforts don't bring you closer to achieving your goals or aren't aligned with your values, you're wasting the precious time you have available. Being strategic about where you spend your time, effort, and money pays dividends. It also means that you get more return on your investment in all areas of life. It's about working smarter, not harder.

Effort must be **intentional** because you need to know what you want from life and how you will get there. Remember the saying: '*If you fail to plan, you plan to fail.*' It's simple. Then, after the plan, you need to execute.

The Universe applauds action, not intention.

I have a crazy busy life, to put it mildly. It's not a complaint by any means. My past actions and compulsive, competitive personality have brought me to this point, and I am grateful for that.

All of the above sounds great until it's put to the test. What happens when things go wrong? In Chapter 3, I mentioned that my failures were a big part of my success, and this wasn't just a catchy tagline. Failure exposes your mindset, values, and whether you mean what you say.

One of my earliest business failures illustrates exactly what I mean.

In 2011, I listed a property that my father-in-law owned at the corner of 291 and 23rd St., Independence, MO. It was a little kiosk that was about 250 sq.ft., located on approximately 30,000 sq.ft. of land. The old saying, *location, location, location,* definitely applied here. The intersection at which it was located had vehicle traffic of approximately 60,000 cars per day.

I listed the property for lease and got a call from a guy named Don Lusaretta. He wanted to put a drive-through-only retail coffee shop at that location. Don was also looking for investors in the business. Coincidentally, I was looking for investment opportunities. With the amount of tenant finish he expected to do and the equipment necessary to start the coffee shop, he was seeking a $40,000 investment, including the purchase of a super-automatic espresso machine. I thought it was a good opportunity, reviewed his business plan, and took the leap. I personally put up about $10,000 of the $40,000 and went to friends and family for the balance.

Don signed a lease, we funded the account, and we were officially in the retail coffee business, called The Daily Grind.

The first issue we encountered was that, except for the first month's rent and security deposit, Don never paid another month's rent. Then, he also never did any of the improvements that were expected. Finally, he never showed us any of the sales numbers. He vanished after putting pressure on him to provide financials and cash register sales reports for our first few months of operation. He took whatever money was in the account and the super-automatic espresso machine. The only things left in the building were some paper cups, lids, and a cash register that you could buy from Sam's Club, which couldn't run sales reports.

It was a disaster from a personal and professional standpoint. Obviously, the thought of losing my investment in the business and watching something with such potential fail was upsetting. However, the potential personal fallout from family and friends who had trusted my judgment and put their hard-earned money into a failed business project was more upsetting.

This is where failure shows a person's true colors. Failure happens to even the most successful people. How you handle it separates those with a growth mindset, a clear set of values and goals, and a long-term plan for success from those without. Failure is a great teacher, if you're willing to learn from it.

It would have been easy to lay the blame elsewhere. My family and friends had access to the same information that I did. I could have reminded them that it was their duty to do their due diligence before investing. I could have pointed the finger at Don, blaming the failure on him for his laziness and unethical behavior. I could have cut my losses, left my family and friends high and dry, and moved on to the next investment without looking back.

That's not how I operate.

Rather than dodging the blame, I took responsibility for what was left when Don took off with everything, and I got to work to turn things around. I wasn't willing to ruin relationships with those I care about over a collective $40,000. Once I had made up my mind, I went to see my father-in-law.

I explained my desire to take on sole responsibility for the kiosk. I asked if I could continue to lease it if I bought out everyone who had invested and continued to operate the business independently. He agreed. Since I didn't have that kind of money just sitting around, I took a personal loan for $55,000. I successfully returned everyone's original investment, roughly $30,000, before putting in another $20,000 to make the necessary improvements and give the business a second chance. Approximately $5,000 remained in the operating account as I ramped up sales.

Before I opened the shop, I spent my weekends meeting with local single-store coffee shop owners to learn as much as I could about the business.

Were they drum-roasting or air-roasting their beans? Where did they get their beans? Were they buying beans already roasted? What syrups were they using? Where did they get their recipes? What was the highest-margin product? The highest-demand product? What were they doing for marketing and loyalty? I wanted to know *everything* about running a successful coffee kiosk.

After meeting with about six individual operators, I realized I could not do this alone. I offered a guy named Ben Helt a management agreement and a branding deal so that I could put up the money, but he would operate the day-to-day business. Ben ran a single-store location in Raytown at the time called Bennetti's. For all practical purposes, this was a second Bennetti's location.

After six months of operation, I went to the shop one day to meet Ben and get the money and financial information for the month. At the time, we were generating about $10,000 per month in gross sales, which is nothing to write home about, but at least we covered payroll and operational expenses.

As I approached the building, I saw a guy in a Scooters Coffee vehicle parked near my kiosk. Scooters was an up-and-coming retail coffee shop that started in Nebraska and was expanding its footprint into the Missouri market. There are currently over 300 Scooters Coffee shops in the Midwest. The gentleman in the car was sitting with a counter in his hand, and I asked if I could help him. He said he was counting traffic, so I asked if Scooters was considering a site in the area. They were, and I immediately saw my exit.

I got into the coffee shop investment with Don because I saw an opportunity for a passive investment. I subsequently bought out my partners and became involved in the operational side of the business to protect my initial investment, but more importantly, my reputation, integrity, and relationships. If I failed, I knew I could make more money in other business ventures.

I never saw this as a franchise opportunity or an investment that fit into my long-term asset portfolio. I was looking for an exit immediately after I bought out my friends and family. The truth is, I thought Ben was my exit, but this opportunity presented itself much sooner than expected.

It was time to cash in on this gamble.

Two months later, I sold the coffee business and assigned the kiosk lease to one of the largest Scooters franchises in the region.

For the record, I did not cut a fat hog on this investment. Did I make a little bit of money? Yes. More importantly, what I did was preserve the relationships of friends and family who trusted me with the Don Lusaretta investment. I was also able to pay my father-in-law over $30,000 in back rent for the months of missed payments per the original lease agreement with Don. I secured my father-in-law a solid long-term tenant with a multi-store operator and a national Scooters franchisee. He is still operating a successful coffee shop at this location today. It was truly turning chicken shit into chicken salad. While I did not *have* to give everyone their money back or pay my father-in-law the back rent Don had signed on for, it was important to me that I did. The entire experience was a good lesson for me.

It exposed what my real values truly are. Repairing and maintaining relationships with friends and family who had lost their investments was more important than money. You can't put a price on that. Showing my father-in-law that I am a man of integrity and taking responsibility for my actions was more important to me than financial advancement. It also showed everyone that I'm always willing to double down on **myself** in my relentless pursuit of success.

Lastly, it was a test of my mindset and positive outlook. I realized that I could learn any industry. There is always room to grow. I learned how to maintain a positive attitude toward an investment that wasn't what I had hoped. I learned how to turn failure into success. Perhaps the biggest lesson I learned is that the people you invest in and the ones you surround yourself with are more important than the business or industry itself.

I spend a lot of my time working hard to hit the milestones I set for myself so I can live up to my full potential. When I use the word "potential," I am not limiting that word to only professional or financial potential, but also potential as a husband, father, friend, philanthropist, etc.

You can have all the best intentions in the world, have the vision board, do the visualizations, and focus on affirmations. Meditate on the future you want. But you need to understand this one simple truth: *You can be on the right track, but if you're not moving forward, you're going to get run over.*

Intention means nothing without action. So, take the action that will lead to fulfilling your vision of your future self and living the life you want to live.

Chapter 5:
Ideas and Strategy for Execution

I bought my first coin laundry soon after I bought my first building. It was located right across the street from the old veterinary clinic that I rehabbed on Independence Ave. The business was a beat-up coin laundromat with 35-year-old equipment and rats the size of a laundry basket. This laundromat, Holiday Laundry, had been in the building for over sixty years and was currently owned by a 75-year-old man who worked the laundromat every single day. The area was a densely populated urban core location, and many of the multi-family buildings in the surrounding areas did not have washer and dryer hookups or laundry facilities in the buildings.

What the existing owner saw as a tired, declining business, I saw as a tremendous opportunity with significant upside potential.

The demographic for this type of business was perfect. While there was some competition in the area, the other laundromats didn't have the building size or parking availability that this location offered. It was a diamond in the rough.

The downside was that it would require a significant cash outlay with an uncertain timeframe to achieve the revenue numbers we needed to generate the desired profit.

Fortunately, I had another friend, John, in the coin laundry business who also loved to help people. He was wealthy enough that if he could help me with money, I could help him by doing the work. It was a win/win situation. There were so many positives.

Now, given my limited cash, I needed to convince my friend of the idea and that the value I would bring was worth partnering on this opportunity.

With the purchase of the business, building, new equipment, and improvements to the building, we were looking at a total investment of over $600,000. In a traditional 50/50 partnership, I would have had to come up with half, which was $300,000. I only had $40,000, so creativity was necessary because I wouldn't do the work for less than a 50/50 partnership. He initially wavered but finally agreed to a deal structure that made us equal partners because I promised that, in addition to my capital contributions, I would run the entire operation, from construction oversight to the day-to-day operations to overall management of the business, at no charge.

It looked like this: we could finance 100% of the equipment, which was $310,000, through the selling vendor's financing and repay this equipment loan from business revenue. That left $290,000 to be financed. I convinced John to initially pay for the building, $290,000, in full and then allow me to borrow $105,000 from a bank, using the free and clear building as collateral. With my $40,000 of savings and my new loan proceeds of $105,000, secured by the building, I paid $145,000 to John as my half of the $290,000 investment capital towards the purchase of the building. We agreed to fund the additional building improvements through laundry revenue.

We would pay ourselves $2,500 a month in rent, for which he would get a $1,250 distribution, and I would get a $1,250 distribution. I would then use my portion to pay my debt service on the $105,000 loan, for which I was solely responsible. Neither of us needed the income from the laundry to live, so we knew that we could reinvest every dollar into covering debt service, marketing, or improving the asset to make it more accommodating to the customers, thus increasing the value of the real estate and the business.

After we closed on the building and business transaction, we immediately ordered all-new equipment. To increase revenue, the simple fact is that you need working equipment; half of the equipment there was tagged off or broken down. The machines in the laundromat were just too old and outdated to do the job well and, in turn, were equally inefficient, thus cutting into margins. When it was time for the new equipment to be delivered, I lived up to my end of the bargain. I went to the laundry after we closed at 10:00 p.m. with my dad and some guys I worked with at UPS, and we took out all of the old equipment. Working into the morning, we loaded up a couple of box trucks full of old equipment and took them to the scrapyard the next day.

We also agreed that the building needed a refresh, with more than just a fresh coat of paint. We started with basic items like adequate heating and air conditioning, proper dryer ventilation for our new dryers, clean working restrooms, more soap options, vending machines, new plumbing for our bulkheads, and more.

I learned a lot from my partner about what customers are looking for when going to a coin-operated laundromat. Things I may not have known to consider if I had gone into the business on my own, like what soaps different ethnicities like to use. Is it kid-friendly, and why would it need to be? How many laundry baskets do we have, and are they easy to move with plenty of spacing in our aisles between machines?

Whenever you are in a competitive landscape in any industry, you need to evaluate what will differentiate you from your competition. Some of the things that I knew we had a beat on were building size as well as parking accessibility and availability. Now, how could we utilize this to drive revenue?

Due to the size of the building, we could offer our customers more seating while waiting for their clothes, so they didn't need to wait in their car. We could also get arcade games in the store to give them and their kids something to do while they wait, while also giving us additional ways to make money. Most people visit laundromats on the weekend and can't afford childcare, so they bring their kids with them. They are typically on the premises for over two hours. Naturally, snacking and drinking sodas are other ways for them to spend more money, so we put in pop and snack vending machines.

For those who didn't want to wait for their clothes, we offered a wash, dry, and fold service, charging by the pound. We already had an attendant on-site to resolve issues, keep the place clean, and keep the customers feeling safe; this was another great revenue generator for us. What other ancillary items could we sell to generate a profit margin? Hangers, soap, dryer sheets, buttons, sewing kits, you name it, we sold it.

The combination of my friend's initial startup knowledge of the laundromat business and my hard work and ability to grow my expertise in marketing, operations, and efficiencies made this deal a home run. When we bought this coin-operated laundry, it generated about $2,500 a week in revenue. By the time all our improvements and changes were implemented, along with marketing efforts, we were generating approximately $7,500 a week 12 months later. We had tripled business in twelve months. This allowed me to set my sights on expanding to another location.

A couple of years later, we picked up another coin-operated laundromat in Kansas City, Missouri, called the "Lost Sock." Although the demographics of the Lost Sock's location were similar to Holiday Laundry, the Lost Sock was a closed and bank-owned laundry. I used the same marketing efforts and new equipment strategy, and freshened up the building to get the Lost Sock back up and running. The biggest difference was that this new building was only 2,400 sq.ft., so I couldn't offer the expanded seating and customer access to arcade games and other amenities.

Other issues included the parking not being as good, fewer machines, and a customer base of zero.

In approximately 12 months, the Lost Sock generated around $2,500 a week. It was not great, but it was not bad, considering the size and equipment mix. Honestly, given the limitations of this building and property, we probably could have generated only about $3,200 to $3,500 per week at most. To our benefit, we had way less cash in and debt on this laundry than the first one, so we could have lower sales numbers and still maintain great returns.

John and I discussed these limitations and considered selling this single-tenant, free-standing Lost Sock building by utilizing a tax-deferred 1031 exchange to purchase another building in the same geographic area that provided a larger store with better parking. If we moved forward with a sale, we would deed restrict the existing real estate to ensure no coin-operated laundry could operate on that property in perpetuity, eliminating competition at this location.

Coincidentally, a building was for sale within two blocks south of the Lost Sock location that was 15,000 sq.ft. and had substantially more parking. There was a national credit tenant in Cash America Pawn, occupying 7,000 sq.ft. The other 8,000 sq.ft. was vacant, a former Car Quest.

It was a single-tenant auto parts store, and most buyers saw it for the previous single-tenant space that it was and the limited number of prospective 8,000 sq.ft. tenants who could utilize the space. With my real estate and construction background, I knew the demand for a smaller space, such as 2,000 sq.ft., would be much higher than 8,000 sq.ft. I also knew we could put a laundromat in 4,000 sq.ft. of the vacancy, thus creating a solid real estate investment deal even before operating the coin-operated laundry itself.

We bought the 15,000 sq.ft. building. We divided the vacant 8,000 sq.ft. into two 2,000 sq.ft. units, one of which we leased to Core Physical Therapy, and the other 2,000 sq.ft. unit we had available for lease. In the remaining 4,000 sq.ft. unit, we constructed a coin-operated laundromat. Once we opened, we immediately generated $3,500 in revenue per week. At its peak, we generated $5,000 a week with increased equipment and parking. In connection with this building, I realized the value of controlling the operating tenant to stabilize a vacant building and create value in the real estate investment. From then on, I started to utilize the businesses I was operating to purchase vacant or distressed investment real estate and create value by stabilizing the property with tenants whose operations I controlled.

I didn't stop there. I located a building that could possibly house a third coin laundry location. We originally looked at the real estate for our third location because it had tremendous upside potential, as it was a 4,800 sq.ft. building right off the highway, with heavy traffic, and only 1,200 sq.ft. leased to Domino's Pizza. I had secured a tenant representation agreement with Fred Loya Insurance in the KC Market, and I knew they were looking for 1,200 sq.ft. in this area. I also knew we could take the remaining 2,400 sq.ft. for a laundromat.

Based on our purchase price and planned improvements, the capitalization rate—or cap rate—on this deal was around 15%, which is almost unheard of in real estate. For those unfamiliar, the cap rate is a way to measure how much income a property is expected to generate annually compared to its cost. To put that in perspective, the average annual return from the stock market typically falls around 8.5%, so a 15% cap rate is exceptionally strong. And that's just the starting point. The return on cash invested and the internal rate of return (IRR), which accounts for both the timing and total value of returns over the life of the investment, would be even higher. And we hadn't even factored in additional income streams yet, like laundry revenue. In short, it was an incredible deal.

I was now using my business income to pay myself rent and leverage the profits to purchase investment real estate. If there was a building that had a vacancy, I knew I could plug my business into it to generate a 25 %+ cash-on-cash return, pay down the principal with debt service, and get my internal rate of return by paying down my principal loan balance over 30% on the real estate. All the while, I pay rent, control the tenant operation, make money as the tenant, and maximize my depreciation benefits from the new equipment.

Now I'm cooking with fire.

I began exploring ways to create efficiencies within the business. Was there any day of the week or time of day when we could operate unmanned to cut labor costs? Water was my biggest expense. What could I do to become more efficient there? I realized that the KCMO water department was charging me per gallon for water going through the meter and charging me the same number of gallons going into the sewer for the sewer charge. That immediately was a red flag because my second biggest expense was gas. I was paying to dry this same water out of the clothes! These commercial washers spin at a very high velocity to extract as much water as possible, but no G-force can dry them completely.

Furthermore, if all of the water did, in fact, come out of the clothes, people wouldn't need to pay to dry their clothes! I challenged the water department on this. They told me to run a study to determine the percentage of water retained in the laundry after the washer's spin rinse. We determined through the study that anywhere between 15-20% of the overall water was not draining out of the machines, depending on the load size and textile material. The water department agreed to discount the sewer portion of my bill by 15%. Sure, I feel that was the low end, but 15% of $6000 in runoff across all three laundries per month is nothing to sneeze at. It put another $10,800 per year in our pocket! According to the KCMO water department, this was the first time anyone had done this.

Even with scaling from operating one coin-operated laundry to three, I still didn't have the economies of scale to hire someone full-time to maintain the equipment, collect the money from the machines, drive to Sam's Club to purchase the snacks, and fill the vending machines. Most of that work still fell to me.

It was around this time that I realized I needed to make a choice about how I wanted to do business in the future. I had to evaluate what I personally was making per hour to operate this business. What was that time costing me in opportunity cost? Was I managing this business portfolio for ½ of what I could make if I redeployed my equity into alternative businesses or real estate transactions? I was at a crossroads and needed to make some decisions about my business path forward.

It was 2016, just five short years after purchasing my first coin-operated laundry. I was working on multi-million-dollar redevelopments, in addition to running the laundromats, ensuring the day-to-day operations ran smoothly. I also had two young kids at home: Bennie, born on Valentine's Day 2014, and Johnny, born in August 2015.

The turning point came one morning in 2016, as I was leaving the laundromat after collecting the money at 5:30 a.m. The money was in a backpack, along with a .38-caliber Smith & Wesson. A police officer pulled me over as I made a U-turn to head to the highway. He asked what was in the bag in the passenger seat, and I told him honestly: money and a gun. After his initial confusion at my response, he asked, Why? I explained that I owned the laundromat up the street and wouldn't collect the cash without protecting myself. Thankfully, he understood and told me to obey basic traffic laws and to get on my way.

That is when I remember thinking to myself that I either commit to growing the coin-operated laundry business so I have six or more locations and can justify hiring a full-time operator, or I sell the businesses immediately. I didn't want to continue to scale if it meant more work for me, and I knew that staying at three locations was not only playing it small but was keeping me tethered to the business instead of allowing me to leverage it into something more.

I thought about my dad and his restaurant business. The challenges inherent in holding and scaling these types of businesses, ones that require a lot of hands-on attention, were more than I wanted to be involved with.

Since the laundry acquisitions, we had put additional cash into improvements from the existing profits, creating value by further increasing the revenue and driving the value of the business up. This created a larger equity position. Equity is the value of the asset minus your total debt.

I realized that while my original cash-on-cash returns were substantial, my IRR was fantastic, and the real estate cap rates were great, my return on equity was diminished and south of 9%. If I could sell this equity and recapitalize the money at 25% cash on cash, why should I keep assets generating only 9%? I could buy, create value, sell, recapitalize, and accelerate the velocity by which I grew my wealth and net worth like nothing anyone has ever seen by continuously turning my cash and recapitalizing my equity.

I had a pregnant wife and two kids at home, and I was heading out at 5:30 am twice a week with a gun to empty washing machines for quarters in a suit and tie and then doing multi-million-dollar redevelopments. The business was a great opportunity to accelerate my wealth accumulation, but it was not one that fit into my future plans. It was a means to an end that had run its course, but not without teaching me valuable business lessons in the process. It was the first time I had scaled a business, and that process taught me some things about myself and how I wanted to approach business going forward.

I was more interested in using the profits from the business to chase bigger opportunities than I was in creating an empire of coin laundries. And so, I decided to sell.

Perhaps the biggest lesson I learned is that I am not one to have an emotional attachment to any building, business, or asset that is purely a utility to make money. This goes against much of what I learned growing up in the Italian community. Many people in the Italian community, as well as the broader business community, have an age-old mentality of buying and holding. Whether it be their house, investment real estate, or business, the idea is that you hold onto things to hand down to the next generation.

I don't believe in generational businesses; I believe in generational wealth!

I now have four kids; do you think that I am going to guide and manage their personalities in businesses they are not passionate about? I'm not going to force my sons or daughter to run the "family" business because that's what someone said should happen 100 years ago. What I wanted was money. I want to grow my net worth so that I can leverage it to grow it even more, and one day, they can do the same. I want to give my kids options, not obligations.

This is when I began viewing all of my assets differently than I had been taught. Instead of return on cash (the actual cash I had invested in the project) or internal rate of return, which even factored in debt paydown, I started looking at assets on a return on equity basis and reevaluated values and equity positions twice a year. As a result, my business strategy became clearer.

At the same time that I had been building the laundromat business, I was scaling up my transaction numbers in commercial real estate at Keller Williams. Time blocking, prioritization, and execution became paramount to being effective while still living according to my values.

In 2012, a lifelong friend of mine, Nate, approached me seeking an opportunity in the brokerage business. I was now forced to evaluate my values and determine what was more important: relationships, helping others close to me, or my success? Despite my rapid growth, bringing Nate on could throw a wrench in my entire structure.

Nate had experienced more than his fair share of adversity. I have known Nate since we were 9 years old, and we became fast and lifelong friends around the age of 12. Nate lost his mom to a battle with cancer when he was 6 years old, which was an extreme blow. He had a very close relationship with his father, and this tragedy brought them even closer together. He never envisioned a life without both of his parents until he was on a scuba trip with his father when Nate was 21, and his dad died right in front of his eyes from complications during the dive. He was now living a life that he never anticipated.

Nate had a strong support system with his older brother and sister and a great web of friends, but no amount of support could bring back his parents or ease the pain that he was suffering.

He faced struggles within himself and was truly down and out at that point in his life. He was heading down the wrong path, and while he hadn't yet hit rock bottom, he was scraping the shit out of the sides. I wasn't at the point where I was ready to grow my team and guide or lead others, but I felt like I needed to help him. First, he's one of my best friends. Second, having come from my own dark place where I was at rock bottom, I knew what it was like and felt for him. I remember talking with my wife about it; she questioned bringing him on under my name. One can understand why. She was just trying to look out for me.

The reality was that I was just now getting my head above water, and trying to save another person simultaneously could sink us both. I wanted to be in a place where I was closing $25 million in annual transaction value before I brought someone else on. This way, I knew that after my company expenses and sustaining my lifestyle at the time, this person would be able to earn a decent enough amount to sustain themselves while working their way up. At the time, I was closing around $18 million in gross transactional volume.

I did bring Nate on, and his performance was a bit like a yo-yo for the first couple of months. He'd perform some days and hit lows the next. Some days, he wouldn't even show up for work. I eventually had to sit him down and have a candid discussion about his commitment to the job. I knew I was committed and needed a team who wouldn't screw around.

Sound familiar? I was having the same types of conversations with Nate that my uncle used to have with me. I began to see my uncle in a different light. I realized that although my uncle didn't bring me back to the company, what he taught me set me up to maximize my true potential. I could never thank him enough for the knowledge, opportunity, and experience that he gave me.

I even considered that he cut me loose for my own benefit, knowing that I could have brought great value to his company in the long term. Maybe he felt that rehiring me for a cushy job would have enabled me to fall back into prior habits. Or maybe he felt the perceived rejection would force me to change my ways.

Over the years, I have worked with my uncle on a number of transactions and still ask for advice if I get stuck. Since I went out on my own, we have played golf, seen each other on holidays, and have a great relationship; he has played a huge part in my success.

I taught Nate several things, much like my uncle taught me. It was time for tough love. If Nate wasn't there on time, he would lose an opportunity and be penalized. He needed to understand the value of time and time blocking. To his credit, Nate took the opportunity to learn and grow.

"Chuck and I have known each other since we were kids. He leads through action, plain and simple. If you won't pick up the phone to make a call and get a listing, he will. If you don't want to "beat the streets," as he put it, to drum up interest in a space or building for sale or lease, he will. If you don't seize the opportunity in front of you, he will, which separates his leadership from anyone else I have worked with.

He doesn't do this to rub it in your face; rather, he does it to motivate you. Too many times, we convince ourselves that it's too tough or it can't be done for one reason or another but to Chuck, the idea that it can't be done is nonsense. He's taught me that opportunities won't wait. If you don't do it, someone else will, so time is of the essence." - Nate Prather

To help Nate focus on developing his skills, I decided that during our work hours, he should only focus on the same handful of things that I prioritized when I went out on my own.

Prospecting: This is the most crucial part of a real estate job, or any sales position, for that matter. This was simply a numbers game; the more calls you make, the more people you prospect, the more meetings you will set, and the more listing agreements or representation agreements you will execute, leading to income potential. Once you have the listings, you prospect for buyers or tenants. Many people stop once they obtain the listing. I taught him that your knowledge and work ethic differentiate you from everyone else. You cannot just put up a sign on the property and wait for someone to call; you must proactively market and prospect, not just reactively respond to interested parties.

Negotiating: This is what differentiates good brokers from great brokers. I needed to teach him how to utilize comparable sales, analytics, deferred maintenance, capital expenditures, various other inspections and overall market knowledge to get the best deal possible for our clients. It is imperative to never put your pocketbook ahead of your clients. Be confident, as this is something that we do every day. If you represent a seller who wants an unrealistic number for his property, you need to tell him what to expect. Just because he wants it doesn't mean it's worth it, and if you don't educate him, you are setting yourself up for failure. If you take a listing at an overpriced number, you are wasting time, money, and resources. Be intentional and realistic; the first negotiation comes with setting clear expectations with your client.

Transacting: Naturally, the busier any broker gets, the more time they spend transacting business. To be the best broker he could be and elevate himself to the next level, he needed to view every deal as transactional. This is a non-emotional industry, purely numbers. If he lost a deal, he needed to get right back on the horse and move on to the next one. I mentioned before that it's a numbers game, and no one, not even me, will execute 100% of the deals they work on.

I once lost a $3 million deal with QuikTrip and a $5 million lease in a building I owned to an international company in the same week. QT couldn't get zoned, and the person who was handling the lease died in a car wreck. That was a life-changing deal for me at the time. I showed up to work the next day at 7 am. Nate told me he didn't know how I did it; he would be in the fetal position.

Closing deals: This is pretty self-explanatory, but it is following through and having closing documents executed in a correct and timely manner, so the money can change hands. Nothing is more annoying than a broker not checking the closing documents and settlement statement until they are sitting at the title company, making corrections that should have been done earlier in the week and finalized prior to the closing. Don't waste anyone's time, especially your clients', and get it right the first time. So many people in this industry don't do this. I would always tell Nate to celebrate the closing, not the contract.

Maintaining Relationships: This is the only part of your day that isn't viewed as transactional, and arguably, it's the most important part. 80% of your business will come from 20% of your clients. Additionally, I explained to Nate that by executing all the above points, he would differentiate himself from others. Opes Commercial Real Estate and its agents/brokers will come in abundance, use our resources, and grow our clients' wealth. We will do so quickly and proactively, and provide professional experience and knowledge that others don't have. These clients will naturally and organically grow their portfolio, which will grow our revenue and income. If you have a *give me everybody once* mentality, you will run out of people to get and eventually be back on 'poor me' island.

Nate eventually got his act together, allowing me to bring on someone who could handle all the administrative duties. It was my second hire. Although Nate was doing better, it was still a battle to keep him on the straight and narrow at times. He seemed to finally hit his stride in 2014, and I felt comfortable bringing a third agent, Cherise, onto the team. She was a seasoned agent with extensive experience, which made the decision easy. It's always easier to recruit existing talent than to have to train new talent.

At the time, I was still operating under the KW umbrella. In 2015, I was finally in a position where I looked at the numbers, and it made more sense for me to break away and continue under my own name than to pay KW commission fees for Nate, Cherise, and me. I already had my broker's license, so everything fell into place as I envisioned when I started out with KW.

I started my own commercial real estate brokerage company, Opes, in May 2015; Nate and Cherise came with me. People asked me why Opes and not my name, as several other commercial real estate companies had done. My response was simple: we've already determined I don't believe in generational businesses, but I also wanted Nate, Cherise, and our team to feel as much a part of Opes as I did.

We were in this together, and it's not just me building this company.

Our team cracked Ingram's book of lists for the first year of Opes Commercial Real Estate in 2016, coming in at number 24. We had sold $35 million in transactional real estate value. Our small team of three has been on this list annually since 2016, with our best year of $70 million in transactional value occurring in 2023, during which I was only involved for half a year. To reward myself for achieving something on that vision board in 2016, I bought myself my first Oxxford handmade suit, another thing on the vision board. When Nate cracked $10 million in transactional value a few years later, I flew him to Chicago and bought him his first Oxxford suit as a reward. Things that were once visions were becoming reality.

If you can dream it, you can achieve it. If you spend your time focusing on all the negatives in your life or possible negatives in the future, you'll multiply your grief. If you focus on practicing gratitude, seeking opportunities, and consistently working toward achieving your goals, you'll receive more opportunities to be even more grateful.

None of it would have been possible if I didn't have my head straight about my values and priorities in life, the mindset that allowed me to believe in my own potential, the goals to keep me on track, and the planning and execution skills to see it all through.

My biggest real estate success story is Nate. By trusting in the time and the methods I taught him, in 2024, he closed over $39.5 million in transactional value! Making money and closing a ton of deals is one thing; changing someone's life and helping them become a leader in their industry, a real contributor to society, and maximizing their potential is by far more gratifying.

Chapter 6:
Leading by Example

"Chuck's passion is obvious and contagious. He pours himself into everything he does. I've worked with Chuck professionally, personally, and philanthropically, and he brings the same go-getter attitude to all aspects of his life. It is inspiring to see Chuck meet every challenge head-on and drive himself and others to success. He makes you want to be better." —Chris Frantze, Partner, Stinson LLP

I hold certain beliefs about leadership and try to emulate these beliefs through my actions. I believe in motivating and inspiring others by example. I am always the first one in the office in the morning. I make a conscious effort to give my full attention and actively listen to people when they speak, to better understand what they are trying to communicate. Sometimes, what people say and the message they're trying to convey are not always the same. I believe in giving people the opportunity to shine, being respectful and understanding, and expressing empathy and compassion. Above all, I believe in consideration. If nothing else, just be considerate. These beliefs form the backbone of my leadership style, a key factor in my business success.

There is a big difference between being a boss and being a leader. Bosses spend their time managing their employees, while leaders spend their time inspiring and empowering their teams to grow, develop, and succeed together.

Characteristic	Boss	Leader
Authority	Relies on positional power to command respect.	Earns respect through actions and character.
Accountability	Blames others for failures.	Takes responsibility for outcomes, good or bad.
Communication	Issues directives: one-way communication.	Engages in open, two-way communication.
Decision-making	Makes decisions independently and enforces them.	Seeks input and fosters collaboration.
Focus	Prioritizes tasks and results.	Balances results with the team's growth.
Growth	Views employees as tools for achieving objectives.	Sees team development as key to success.
Inspiration	Motivates through fear or incentives.	Inspires through vision and shared goals.
Recognition	Focuses on faults and shortcomings.	Recognizes and celebrates achievements.
Relationships	Maintains a hierarchical, transactional approach.	Builds trust and nurtures meaningful connections.
Risk-taking	Avoids risks to maintain control.	Encourages innovation and calculated risks.
Rules	Enforces rules rigidly.	Adapts rules to empower and engage the team.
Support	Expects employees to handle challenges on their own.	Actively supports and mentors team members.
Vision	Focuses on short-term goals and immediate tasks.	Guides with a long-term vision and purpose.

We are traditionally taught that the golden rule is to treat others as we want to be treated. This rule needs some tweaking. Instead of treating others the way *you* want to be treated, treat them the way *they* want to be treated.

This is a seemingly simple yet powerful change. So many people get this part wrong because we are taught to "treat others the way you want to be treated." Although I can appreciate the sentiment, not everyone wants to be treated the way I like to be treated.

The concept of the change is "consideration." That's really all it takes. All any of us wants is to have our wants and needs considered. When you are considerate of someone else's needs, including their specific communication style, you'll be far more effective in getting what you both want and need.

This shift emphasizes empathy and understanding, key traits of an effective leader. These are traits I always strive to live by. By recognizing and respecting the unique needs, preferences, and motivations of each member of my team, I am able to foster a more inclusive and motivating environment, which makes the environment more profitable for all involved.

I do this by getting to know my team members and understanding their needs. I learned how to do this in an unconventional way–by learning to better communicate with my wife! *The 5 Love Languages* book by Dr. Gary Chapman is a book that my wife and I used to better understand each other's needs and communication styles, but I realized that it could also apply to leadership, obviously using different criteria than those used for romantic relationships!

The key message is understanding what makes your team members feel appreciated at work. For example, some people want to hear words of praise when they complete tasks, while others prefer public recognition in a company newsletter. Some team members prefer a monthly one-on-one meeting, while others feel empowered by being given more space and autonomy to do their thing. Understanding which method to employ with each person in a way that suits their preferences is key to treating them how *they* want to be treated rather than adopting a one-size-fits-all approach.

Ask yourself whether the tactics you employ are the most effective suited to the unique person with whom you're communicating. And, if you're not sure how best to approach them, ask! It's as simple as that. Remember to be open, honest, sincere, and respectful. You can't go wrong with this recipe.

Consideration + Effort = Winning Recipe

I appreciate the effort, no matter how big, small, or seemingly irrelevant. Whether in youth sports, at home, or in the workplace, you must complete the task and put forth the effort. There is a saying that "Productivity is never an accident." Another saying I embrace is: "The activity or action produces the result."

Nothing great has ever been achieved without an equally great amount of effort put into it. What you put in will always determine what you get out. It's simple: No growth will happen if you don't put the necessary effort into driving your business and the people you employ. On the contrary, you might move backward, and that's never a direction any business aims to go. Most things in life take some level of effort. Relationships take effort; remaining healthy takes effort; building a business takes effort; improvement at games, sports, or anything takes effort, and you have to be intentional to maximize your results in all facets of your life.

Winston Churchill said, "Continuous effort–not strength or intelligence–is the key to unlocking our potential."

If you quit putting effort into something, it will wither and die. You have control over the effort you exert on a daily basis. So, if you're not putting in enough effort to improve or make something successful, that's on you. No one else can put forth the effort for you. That's your personal responsibility. I never expect more from anyone else than I expect out of myself, and I don't ask anyone to do anything I wouldn't be willing to do myself.

It's a necessary ingredient for leaders. You set the tone for your team by leading from the front.

Leading from the front is about visibility and participation. You don't want to get too far ahead of your team, or they will lose sight of the vision; that's why visibility and participation are imperative. Being down in the trenches with your team, demonstrating commitment and solidarity, and not barking orders from behind your expensive desk. You can't be a leader by separating yourself from the very important people who pump blood into your business. Leading from the front not only builds trust but also sets a powerful example of accountability and dedication.

When team members see me working alongside them, sharing their challenges, and committing to their goals, it inspires confidence and encourages a shared commitment to our business's success. At the end of the day, it is a partnership just like any other.

Do the tedious and monotonous jobs that your employees do for you daily. Show them that you are not above such jobs and motivate them by saying, *Let's go do this* instead of just *Do this!* You read what I did when I bought the coin laundromats!

When I expanded my business portfolio to include a cannabis company, I also put in the work. I visited the facility and learned from the employees about their pain points and how we could better assist them in improving their performance, automating tasks, and making their jobs more efficient. I made it clear that I was invested not just in the company's success but in the success of everyone who worked for it. Spending time talking to people and doing the types of tasks that I usually don't do but are the backbone of the company helped me better understand what employees at all levels needed. It also helped them see that I actually care about more than the bottom line.

Motivation is the engine of productivity, but its fuel is inspiration. As a leader, my ability to inspire my teams is crucial. That means conveying a clear vision, communicating passionately, and showing genuine enthusiasm for the organization's goals and values. It also means being transparent about challenges and showing how each team member's effort contributes to overcoming those challenges.

Here are a few strategies to enhance motivation and inspire your team:

- **Professional Growth**: One of the most important things a leader can provide for their team is the opportunity for professional development. When team members feel they are growing and learning, their engagement and productivity rise. I am obsessed with getting better every day and supporting constant development. A year ago, I hired Action Coach, an in-person and online training program designed for our executive-level and leadership teams to further develop them as leaders. A good leader isn't intimidated by the growth and development of others; they encourage it and grow right alongside it.

- **Empowerment**: Give team members autonomy over their tasks. Empowerment fosters innovation and improves job satisfaction. Few people like to be micromanaged. When your team believes you trust their abilities, they rise to the challenge.
- **Recognition**: Regularly acknowledge individual and team achievements. Recognition reinforces positive behaviors and outcomes, and just makes people feel good.
- **Purpose**: Connect daily tasks with broader organizational goals. When people understand the 'why' behind their work, they are more likely to invest fully in the 'how.' Nobody wants to feel like they're engaged in busy work or checking boxes. Help your team understand the value in everything they do for the organization.
- **Positive Influence:** Cultivating a culture of respect, encouragement, continuous collaboration, and improvement will have a positive influence at every level of the business. This culture encourages team members to take the initiative to innovate, knowing their contributions will be supported and valued.

Remember, the greatest leaders don't just create followers; they cultivate new leaders. The greatest compliment any teacher can receive is the student outperforming the teacher.

"Chuck's influence on my leadership style has been profound, particularly in three key areas: adaptability, continuous improvement, and decisive decision-making. His emphasis on adaptability has taught me to navigate through dynamic environments with flexibility and resilience, ensuring that I can adjust strategies and approaches as circumstances evolve.

Chuck's relentless pursuit of improvement has instilled in me a mindset of constant learning and growth, driving me to seek out opportunities for enhancement in both myself and my team. Additionally, his model of decisive decision-making has empowered me to make tough choices swiftly and confidently, understanding the importance of decisive action in leadership. Overall, Chuck's impact has equipped me with the tools and mindset necessary to lead effectively in an ever-changing landscape." —Jim Mozena, Elevation Cannabis, CFO

Effective communication is an essential skill for great leadership. The inability to effectively communicate your wants, needs, hopes, desires, emotions, thoughts, and boundaries leads to misunderstandings, missed opportunities, and emotional pain or misalignment.

Since the COVID-19 pandemic and technological advancements, communication and learning have shifted to devices and digital platforms. People have lost what it means to have effective personal communication. Much of what makes life challenging or causes challenges in business and personal relationships stems from ineffective communication, which often results from a lack of early communication development.

Effective communication is the cornerstone of any relationship, whether personal or business. In business, it is a crucial tool necessary for building trust, encouraging teamwork, and driving overall organizational success. At its core, effective communication involves not only speaking and active listening but also the ability to identify and understand nonverbal cues, as well as providing clear, concise, helpful, and respectful feedback.

No matter how hard we wish we could, none of us possesses the ability to read another's mind. Yet, we so often expect others to do just that. How often have you heard someone say, *"Well, I shouldn't have to say it. They should just know that's what I meant. It's obvious."* A prime example of poor communication leading to a failure of communication.

No one knows what you're thinking. In reality, every one of us is so caught up in our own thoughts, problems, and lives that we rarely pause to consider whether we've communicated a message, task, or instruction in the most effective manner possible. Being an effective communicator is essential to being a leader.

Effective communication sets you apart from the crowd, especially in business.

I've seen companies inhibit their growth and even collapse because their systems and internal communication processes were nearly non-existent. I've seen management lose top performers because they lacked the effective communication skills to hold onto valuable employees. What's so frustrating is that it's completely unnecessary because these skills can be taught and learned. They are vital for building trust and relationships in any team, whether at work or home. Let's look at some of the most important elements of communication.

- **Be Clear and Concise:** So much of what we try to communicate often gets lost in the noise. You want to communicate your message in a way that is easily understood, avoiding complex language or detours that might leave someone feeling a bit confused. Avoid fluff and just be open, direct, and honest.

- **Active Listening:** Active listening means seeking to understand what the other person is trying to communicate. It is not just hearing the words being spoken, but listening to tone, inflection, and watching body language. An example of a failure of active listening is simply hearing the speaker and waiting for them to finish their sentence, so you can talk. That's listening to respond. Active listening involves not just *hearing* what is being said but *understanding* the underlying message and emotions that are driving the message. You can practice active listening by nodding to show someone you're listening to them. Repeat back what you hear and understand, and then ask them to confirm whether that is what they meant to communicate to ensure you've understood them correctly.

- **Nonverbal Communication:** Much of what we communicate is never said in words. Nonverbal cues, such as body language, tone of voice, and facial expressions, communicate far more than words ever can. Being perceptive of these cues can help you identify when someone is failing to communicate what they intended. We often try to hide behind our words, but nonverbal communication never lies. On that note, scrolling on your phone, multi-tasking, looking around, or fidgeting are nonverbal cues that show disinterest and can negatively impact communication with others.

- **Constructive Feedback:** It is essential for growth and constant improvement both in our personal and professional lives. Without feedback, we have no way of knowing what we need to change to do better. An effective leader provides feedback that is specific, actionable, and respectfully delivered. There's an art to giving feedback in a way that helps someone improve. It hinges mostly on your ability to identify and understand two things: (1) What drives someone? and (2) To what type of communication do they respond most favorably? Seek the most effective driver to help incentivize your people to do their best.

- **Coach for Enthusiasm:** Effective communication involves coaching your team to generate enthusiasm. If you drive and push them, you will generate fear, which will shackle them. Get in the trenches and show how it's done when there is a breakdown; don't just point the finger. When things go right, give credit where it is due and say "we." Don't take credit and say "I." There are no growth companies with one employee.

Clear and effective communication is essential for team collaboration. When team members are encouraged to communicate clearly and effectively, they can share their ideas, devise creative solutions to problems, and make decisions more efficiently. This level of communication is the driving force of innovation. It allows team members to feel safe and motivated to express their thoughts and opinions without fear of ridicule or retribution. Creativity and innovation cannot exist in a stifled environment. Clear and effective communication ensures everyone is on the same page and aiming at the same goal while reducing misunderstandings and conflicts that can easily derail a project.

A leader who prioritizes clear and effective communication can ensure that strategic goals are properly articulated and that everyone within the company understands their specific role in helping achieve these goals. When everyone is aligned with the task at hand, a team can reach its goal faster.

I have weekly meetings with my executives, upper management, and director-level positions at all my companies. We have quarterly alignment meetings to develop a 90-day strategy and weekly meetings to ensure we stay on course to achieve those goals. This ensures constant communication and allows us to course-correct and be proactive in changing direction. I encourage the team to attend these meetings and communicate what is working and what is not working sooner rather than later. As we have grown and developed a more aligned strategy with fewer rapid changes, we have transitioned these to biweekly meetings to be conscious of everyone's time.

All high-performing individuals and leaders are able to be open to and truly listen to both positive feedback and constructive criticism. The average person finds the latter extremely challenging. Accepting constructive criticism can be tough for the ego to accept at times. The reality is that even if you're at the top of your game (especially when you're at the top of your game), you need as much constructive criticism as possible so you know what you need to change and improve in order to perform optimally. You can pick any high-performing individual in any field you want, and I guarantee that they have a mindset focused on constantly seeking feedback from different sources that will help them learn something valuable they can implement in their lives to better themselves in some way.

I want to highlight that not all feedback is helpful. If you're going to seek feedback or advice, it needs to be from someone who has achieved what you are still aiming for, someone who knows more than you and has more experience than you do, and someone who is an expert in their field. Ideally, it's from someone aligned with your values, goals, and aspirations, with a growth mindset.

There is a parable about good feedback, which is like the nugget of gold in the bucket of sand that is thrown at your face. The sand stings, but once you wash the grit out of your eye and wipe away the criticism or feedback that isn't helpful, you should be able to find the small nugget of gold that really means something.

I have always valued feedback. Sometimes it may take working with a therapist to really build this strength. There continues to be a stigma around people attending or receiving advice from a licensed therapist when going through difficult times in their lives. In fact, it is a valuable personal development tool designed to help individuals enhance themselves and their relationships.

When you see a therapist, you are consulting with someone who has been trained to help you get to the root cause of a problem in your life.

You learn so much about yourself, and it allows you the opportunity to take a step back, assess thought processes and behavioral responses that might not be particularly helpful in your life, and do the personal work that will help bring about positive changes.

People often avoid therapy because we fear taking a good look in the mirror while identifying and accepting the not-so-pretty parts of ourselves and, more importantly, accepting personal responsibility to do something about it, Ego Strength. What do most of us do when we fear something? We run away, lock it inside, or throw judgment at it – so we don't have to face it!

I embrace humility because I am certain that I do not know all there is to know. I am smart enough to know that I am not that smart. I know that a team can do more than one person alone. I know that a strong team can do more than a team made up of people who shouldn't and don't want to be there. If I make a mistake, I will always own up to it. I've encountered too many egotistical people in my life at my level who think they know everything. Allowing your ego and insecurities to run rampant is counterproductive and limiting.

I will be the first to admit when I made a decision that didn't work. This is a huge factor when motivating those to whom you delegate. I do not instantaneously put the blame on them. I first examine the strategy, and if it's faulty, I don't continue to try to force a square peg into a round hole; I quickly pivot to execute a different strategy.

Being humble is part of being different. Being different is not a bad thing or a weakness to avoid; it's a strength. It takes courage, optimism, and vision to be different. When everyone else is zigs, don't be afraid to zag. I love ideas, even if they don't get executed. I like when my management team collaborates and brainstorms ways to present what makes us different from others to our employees, community, and customers on what makes us different compared to others. Why us? Why our business? Why should our customers, clients, or community trust that we'll do a better job than anyone else?

I also believe in giving credit where credit is due and doing so generously. If someone did a good job, acknowledge it by telling them so. Encourage others to continually strive for improvement. I appreciate that even the smallest amount of progress is better than none. So, I praise my people when they perform well and when they improve, not only in their jobs but in their personal lives as well.

A strong leader understands that you need to take care of the people who work for you so they can take care of your business. Sir Richard Branson is a business pioneer who has always understood this pivotal concept. He said, *"Clients do not come first. Employees come first. If you take care of your employees, they will take care of the clients."* In other words, make sure your own house is in order first. What my employees think of my leadership is the best gauge of how I'm really doing.

"Chuck has the ability, like no one I have ever worked with, to surround himself with not just good people but the right people. He has a vision of not just where the organization is going to be in 6 months, 2 years, or even 5 years, but more importantly, how his teams will operate in order to achieve those goals. Everyone always claims they are a good listener. They take notes or give acknowledgments when you are around these individuals, but I promise you one thing.... There is no one I have ever worked with who listens as well as Chuck. I do believe the most important quality that makes him successful is his compassion for those around him, whether it be his friends or employees. He makes sure that everyone who was a part of the success or achievement has a seat on the bus." - Bo Thomas, VP of Operations, Specialized Home Care

Testimonials from my team members serve as proof of what you can achieve when you lead from the front. I know that my actions impact those around me, whether in business or my personal life. However, influence goes both ways–how I treat others and the example I set will influence those around me, just as the people I surround myself with will significantly impact my life. It is, therefore, not just necessary but vital that we all take inventory of both regularly.

To be an exemplary leader and live a life by design, you need to identify your strengths and weaknesses. It's good to know what you're good at, but it's even more important to know what you're bad at so you can either upskill or delegate.

If you can't delegate and empower the right people to do tasks that need doing, you're the wrong person to be in a leadership position. Our saying, "You need to delegate to elevate," stands as proof of this, and it's something that I am very passionate about. I don't *want* to and can't do everything by myself. I want to be productive at a high level, not just busy.

I want a team I can rely on to get the job done. I also know that it is my responsibility to lead from the front and show them the way while giving them enough agency and autonomy so they don't feel micromanaged or stifled. This allows them to do their job to the best of their ability. You'll know if a task is not getting done if you keep your finger on the pulse. It'll show when your Key Performance Indicators (KPIs) are not being met, or the numbers don't reflect what you've set out to achieve. On the retail side, you'll see it in terms of the quality of your systems, staffing, and sales. I've seen too many people in management positions who micromanage their teams because they do not trust their people to do what needs to be done.

If the task or project can be done by anyone else, doesn't need your approval or expertise, and won't do too much damage if done incorrectly, delegate it! You want to do what others do, but in less time. That's only possible when you are good at delegating and managing people. Then, knowing you have the right people on your team to make it happen, you can move forward faster than your competitors.

Everyone is different, with different needs and motivational drivers. As a leader, it's your job to figure out those drivers and help the person in front of you develop into the best possible version of themselves.

All the points I've mentioned here are crucial in my experience. But, above all, you need to practice what you preach. You cannot say, "*Do as I say and not as I do.*" That's not congruent with good leadership. You need to lead yourself the same way you lead others. With compassion, motivation, consideration, and always seeking to identify the areas where you need to improve.

Chapter 7:
Scaling Up

Earlier, we covered some key foundations of effective leadership and goal setting. We talked about how aligning your goals with your values brings clarity and purpose, helping you stay focused. Then, we delved into turning ideas into action, exploring strategies for making things happen. We also explored the importance of leading by example and how your actions can influence your team. With all that in place, it's time to think about scaling up—taking everything you've learned and expanding your impact for sustainable growth and lasting success.

I previously mentioned that scaling up for me was about accelerating my net worth, not generational businesses. Everything is for sale except my wife and kids. Too often, people get emotionally attached to businesses, real estate, or other appreciating or even depreciating assets because they are not honest with themselves about the valuation and end up riding that horse down to zero.

One of the very first real estate deals I did when I got out of prison was with a buddy of mine named Frank Termini. Frank was a physical therapist by trade and a damn good one at that. He and I grew up in the same neighborhood and went to the same college. I even used Frank's ID as a fake when I was below the age of 21 to gamble in casinos.

In 2011, Frank started his first physical therapy clinic, Core Physical Therapy, in a 600 sq.ft. space in Liberty, MO. He was very clinical and a great physical therapist, one I had previously used for my own personal rehab. But Frank was not a businessman. Not only did he not understand how to grow, but he also had no idea how to evaluate staffing or utilization inefficiencies in his clinic. I can honestly say that I don't even know if Frank knew whether he was making money in his business or not.

After his ability to treat, Frank's next best skill was his ability to sell. He could visit a surgery center or an orthopedic surgery clinic, speak with case managers or referring nurses, and walk out with a handful of referrals. He had great relationships with orthopedic surgery groups and knew how to tailor a treatment plan to maximize outcomes for the patient, which positively reflected on the surgeon. He knew what he was talking about in the treatment sense and was growth-oriented from a sales perspective. He could get the business, but he needed to know how to maximize monetization without being a treating therapist. He needed to be a leader of other therapists.

Frank came to me one day looking for money to assist in growth. When I asked him his strategy and how he would utilize the money, he had no idea.

Was it simply growing the Liberty, MO, clinic into a larger footprint to serve more patients? Was it expanding into multiple brick-and-mortar locations? What was his target demographic? Was he going to enter retail buildings like Select Physical Therapy and SERC as part of a marketing strategy to drive high-volume traffic with signage? Was he going to get the staff referrals? What equipment did he need? How many clinics did he want? What was his exit strategy?

He didn't have the answers to any of the questions I asked him; he just knew he wanted to expand into multiple brick-and-mortar locations, have the ability to hire staff, and have enough money to cover the increased payroll.

Frank wasn't negotiating reimbursement rates with his insurance carriers, nor did he know how to maximize the floor space at each location. His mentor—a good friend of my family—had successfully exited his own physical therapy business years earlier by selling a three-clinic operation to a larger company. I met with him to strategize the best approach and ensure that Frank understood the plan. Ultimately, any buyer was looking for a strong presence on the map, but we needed to be strategic in our approach. We had to avoid placing clinics too close to a potential buyer's existing locations while ensuring they were near hospitals and key referral sources to maintain high patient volumes.

We laid out our vision and direction for Core PT to grow to three clinics, engage a consultant, and then sell the business. I felt I could assist Frank with no more than three clinics since this was not my primary focus. I was already juggling other business interests and a growing family. Without a vision, no one is going anywhere. It's essential to know your vision before you can effectively communicate it. You need to identify it for yourself first. Then, articulate the core values, objectives, and outcomes you want to achieve. The vision should be specific, measurable, and compelling enough to inspire others.

Shortly after I invested in Core Physical Therapy, we opened a second clinic in Gladstone, MO, directly adjacent to an orthopedic surgery center. That location created great synergy and a built-in referral base for us, allowing Frank to maintain his position in one of the clinics as we began searching for a third clinic, which we ultimately found in Independence, MO, through an acquisition. We relocated it to a better location and opened a fourth clinic.

Once we had four clinics, Frank was out selling for all of them and was no longer a treating therapist. We sought to position the business to sell because we anticipated our revenue would decrease due to insurance provider payments for physical therapy services decreasing, while the salaries for physical therapists were going up. We understood that unless we were willing to deploy significant capital to grow and scale up the business, which we were not, we would get eaten from within.

We sought to maximize revenue at these existing locations for the next year to build a solid trailing twelve-month financial record to present to a potential buyer for our exit from the business. We hired the same consulting company my family friend had engaged years before his exit, which was Paul Martin Healthcare Advisors. They helped clean up our operation and financial reporting to present to possible purchasers. We ultimately sold the clinic to Select Medical, a nationally recognized healthcare provider, marking a successful exit and a significant milestone in our growth journey.

Around the same time I initially invested in Core PT, Frank had also started a home health company, Specialized Home Care, with another friend of his, Erik, from PT school. They were grossly undercapitalized, given that the revenue for services performed by this company came from Medicare, and the gap in time between the provision of the service and the payment from Medicare was significant. This delay required Specialized Home Care to maintain sufficient capital to fund its operations, including payroll, while waiting for payment from Medicare. They also needed money to buy out two non-operational partners who had sweat equity but never put in the sweat.

In 2015, Frank came to me and requested help with Specialized Home Care as well. I reached out to another buddy of mine, with whom I have transacted many real estate and business dealings. As a matter of fact, he is the millionaire I mentioned earlier who got his start selling salvaged freight out of the trunk of his car. PJ and I looked at this investment opportunity. We bought out the two non-operational partners and immediately put money into the company for maintaining expenses for operations, which gave us about 20% of the company.

The year after we bought in, Specialized Home Care had a gross revenue of $2.6 million with one office in Independence, MO, and approximately 40 employees. We knew that to grow revenue, we needed to continue reinvesting profits in the company and expand our patient coverage area and office footprint. To achieve this, we opened an office in Leawood, Kansas.

When we opened new offices, reimbursement was delayed until accreditation was completed, temporarily suspending all owner distributions. Frank and the other business partner, who relied on these distributions for their income, faced a cash crunch. In response, they sought to sell additional equity in the company to weather the delay and maintain the lifestyle to which they were accustomed. While not intentional, this situation allowed PJ and me to acquire an additional 30% of the company, making all four of us equal partners.

PJ and I saw the home health space as a fantastic investment opportunity. With 86% of our revenue coming from Medicare reimbursements—essentially guaranteed government money—we had financial stability from the accounts receivable perspective. However, this also meant facing heavy regulatory challenges, including audits that could create operational hurdles. Fortunately, we had a strong operator leading the company.

While Frank focused on driving sales referrals for both Home Health and outpatient PT clinics, Bo Thomas, our VP of Operations, leveraged his extensive home health experience from a previous role to keep things running smoothly. Through Bo's hard work, dedication, and commitment to growing Specialized Home Care, he was able to secure sweat equity in the company, and we presented him with an incentivized comp plan. This is part of taking care of those who take care of your business.

In 2018, we hit $6.5 million in annual gross revenue. We wanted to expand again in Wichita, Kansas. That same year, we received an unsolicited offer to sell our company from Lorient Capital, a private healthcare equity firm based in Detroit, Michigan. This private healthcare equity firm, or PE, had essentially offered us an equivalent to our top-line revenue. However, as the due diligence and the transaction progressed, they got cold feet and tried to re-trade the deal. We told them we weren't interested in a renegotiation and would continue to scale the business and drive the value up. It had no effect on me, as I'm a non-emotional operator and investor, strictly transactional. I learned a long time ago that in real estate, you celebrate the closing, not the contract.

However, the other owners within our company had seen the value we could have gotten, and they only thought about selling.

Shortly after the decision to continue scaling up in 2019, COVID-19 hit, shutting down the continuum of care facilities, hospitals, and all elective surgeries. This resulted in a drop in revenue from approximately $6.5 million annually to $5.2 million. It also had a significant effect on our outpatient PT Clinics, as we were heavily reliant on elective surgeries. Frank and Erik were tired, and now they saw value and revenue drop due to circumstances outside our control. The other owners felt that PJ and I made the wrong decision to hold and continue to scale instead of turning it over to the PE firm, even at the discounted price they wanted to pay us, and they wanted out.

We saw their eagerness to sell as another opportunity to further invest the revenues in the company, jump into the Wichita market, and start a hospice company. It would act as a natural bridge to in-home aging and end-of-life care.

We recruited Kathryn, the daughter of my family friend who had helped us in the Core PT expansion, as another seasoned operational and business development person. She was a strong-willed physical therapist by trade, but very business-oriented and could sell a ketchup popsicle to a woman in a white dress. She had experience in hospital-owned home health operations, outpatient physical therapy, and managing a handful of SERC Physical Therapy clinics, which helped her from an operations perspective. She knew the business, quality of care, sales, and efficiencies. I don't want to say the transition was seamless, but the learning curve was accelerated under Bo's guidance and with Kathryn's drive and motivation.

Home Health in Wichita took off under her guidance. She was getting as many Medicare referrals in her first month as our sales reps in Kansas City, who had 15 years of experience and relationships.

PJ, Bo, Kathryn, and I bought the rest of Frank and Erik's stock in 2020 at the valuation previously offered by the PE. We began scaling horizontally and sought to grow vertically, offering full in-home and in-facility aging in place services.

Again, because we didn't rely on income from this company to cover our living expenses, we could reinvest all profits into scaling both the hospice and home health businesses. We saw this as a great opportunity for growth and expansion. By 2022, we had built a strong team, ramped up sales, and put the Covid pandemic behind us.

The home health company continued to grow with a top-line revenue of $8.7 million in 2022. It ultimately generated over $10 million in revenue in 2023 before we sold Specialized Home Care in August of 2024. With the earnout structure over the next couple of years, this could be over an eight-figure exit. It was a huge win for us, nearly doubling the sale price that the PE company had offered us years earlier.

We retained the hospice side of the business, but still hadn't quite figured out how to make money in hospice. Previous industry experts told us that we would be breaking even at a 30 average daily census, referred to as *ADC*, which means that we average 30 people in care per day per month. We far exceeded this census, yet we were still managing to lose money.

On multiple occasions, we hired directors or executives with hospice experience to run our hospice company, and each one proved to be a failed experiment. We decided to stop the turnover carousel and let our people step in and attempt to juggle hospice.

Kathryn and Bo were running both companies without knowledge or experience in hospice before the home health transaction. We needed to start to compartmentalize our businesses and find the right people from outside our organization to focus strictly on the growth and operations of the hospice business. The sale of Specialized Home Care forced us to do so, as the buyer required both Kathryn and Bo to remain with Specialized Home Care with additional bonuses and earnouts tied to their employment status.

We spun off the hospice company and rebranded it as Elevate Hospice. At the time of the transaction, we were up to a 90 ADC and losing more money than at a 30 ADC. People would tell us that the ADC creates the enterprise value, but I didn't want enterprise value; I wanted income.

We had already been involved in this experiment for two years, with three failed operators, and we had lost roughly $2 million through this startup venture. No acquirer would buy a 90 ADC that was losing money. Our trailing 12-month financials reported a top-line revenue of $4.5 million, yet we incurred a loss of $800,000. I wanted to figure out why, but I had reached a point where I didn't have time. PJ was ready to throw in the towel, but I wanted one more shot to make money and make this work before we simply sold the company and salvaged whatever monetary value we could for license value.

This hospice company was stuck in startup/scale-up mode, and we didn't have the right people in the right seats. We had Bo and Kathryn operating in hospice, but they had no operational experience. We were operating hospice contrary to everything I had ever told myself.

Sometimes, even highly skilled employees may lack the necessary bandwidth or the right director-level leadership to effectively manage their teams and drive growth within their department or the business. Sometimes, you may be able to identify that a certain employee is in the wrong job. They applied for and are working in an administrative position, but because you pay attention and are involved in all aspects of your business, you can recognize that they show strong creative skills. They're clearly not feeling fulfilled in their admin job, so why not put them in a role where they can express their strengths, which will help them feel more motivated? It's a win-win.

I have my teams take individual assessments of their strengths and weaknesses, and each team is evaluated quarterly. I do this across every company and have brought a consultant on full-time to assist with oversight.

When we were forced to delineate the two companies, I had no choice but to find someone with extensive experience who knew how to operate the hospice company. We no longer had the ability to continue carrying the financial deficit that the hospice was creating. It was time to seek talent and recruit them rather than simply posting jobs and hiring. We wanted the best operator, not interviewer. I met with a couple of people with a lot of hospice business experience, looking for an opportunity to invest in themselves and the company's growth.

They spoke my language. One handled operations, and one handled business development. I structured an employment agreement and comp plan to give them equity opportunities based on revenue, census, and profit margin, all at a locked-in valuation so their growth wouldn't affect their option to secure their equity position. At the time of writing, I am six months into the agreement. We have hit every equity metric, and they are fully capitalized in the company. We are over 200 ADC, and our forward-looking 2025 projections show a topline revenue of over $10 million, with close to 25% going to the bottom line.

Know what you know and know what you don't know.

Before 2022, I would have spent as much time as I had available to find out what I needed to do and how I needed to do it to assist in aligning hospice operations and ensuring it was profitable. I have a wife, four kids, and multiple business ventures. I coach three Little League baseball teams, and I'm the CEO of a vertically integrated cannabis company in three states with over 600 employees. I needed to maintain a position and not lose sight of this large-scale business operation, so I had to recruit and hire the best talent I could find in my other ventures. So, that's what I did, even if it meant giving them an opportunity at equity.

You can't spend percentages; all you can spend is money. What good was it having a larger percentage of a company or real estate asset losing money every month when I could have a smaller percentage of something making me money every month?!

Throughout my career, I have heard people say, What does he know about coin laundromats? What does he know about retail coffee shops? What does he know about outpatient physical therapy? Home health? What did you know about your first job when you started, or your second? I knew nothing about commercial real estate when I started.

These people are missing the point. It's not always what you know going into the opportunity. It's what you're willing to learn, the time you're willing to spend to gain knowledge and expertise in that field, and the people you put in place to run the day-to-day activities within these businesses.

How do I create value? My value is based on my ability to evaluate the market dynamics in a particular sector as a whole and identify potential growth opportunities. I must understand the constraints and limitations, regardless of whether it's real estate, laundromats, coffee shops, physical therapy, home health, hospice, cannabis, hospitality/social clubs, professional employment organizations, etc. I also create value by locating and recruiting the best talent to operate the company and the best person to lead business development for our value proposition.

The right people in the right seats.

I pride myself on doing what I say I will do, building a great culture, and empowering people to lead while leading and guiding them. Letting them be managed, but not micromanaged. Because of this, I'm able to secure high-level talent, and that's what has helped me scale and grow.

As businesses scale, it's important to recognize that growth doesn't always mean just expanding vertically. To truly unlock greater potential, companies often find it beneficial to branch out into new ventures, growing horizontally before scaling up again. This approach still relies on core business fundamentals—creating operational efficiencies, maximizing revenue, and minimizing risk. A key element in this process is considering the business's exit strategy early. By planning for potential future buyers or transitions from the outset, businesses can build a stronger foundation for both immediate success and long-term expansion, positioning themselves for even greater opportunities ahead.

Chapter 8:
Terrapin Scare Station

In 2018, Missouri passed a constitutional amendment legalizing marijuana for medical purposes. The state intended to issue 60 cultivation licenses, 90 manufacturing licenses, and 192 retail dispensary licenses, with 24 of the dispensary licenses in each of the state's eight congressional districts. It was a limited license opportunity where licenses would be awarded by a redacting scoring system to be scored by a third party.

As part of the rules and regulations, the State would require 51% of the money for cannabis license application investments into the facilities come from Missouri residents. The Division of Cannabis Regulation also required operational experience from out-of-state operators. Part of the application process included a non-refundable application fee per license application, to be paid to the state, which was fully at risk, as not every applicant would receive a license. When applying, the applicant had to have both the location for the cannabis operations secured and proof of funds on the capital side to build out and commence the operations. Missouri required proof of funds of $500,000 for dispensary and manufacturing applications, and $10 million for cultivation applications.

I put together a group of four investors through Opes Capital, LLC, who would assist in upfront at-risk capital to apply for the licenses through Terrapin Investment Fund IV, LLC. Due to the increased risk taken by this investor group, we received a Class B share of stock in Terrapin Investment Fund IV, LLC. We anticipated raising additional capital from other investors once we, or if we, were awarded licenses, and those other investors would receive a different Class A share of stock. Distributions would be distributed to these classes of shares on a waterfall scenario, with the A Share class receiving the majority of the waterfall until they received all of their money back. Over time, the more money the A Share class received the lesser percentage they would receive in distributions. This waterfall would allow the B class, who had increased risk initially, to benefit from larger gains in the backend, should success ensue.

The costs provided by this initial four-person investment group included application fees, costs to acquire potential real estate for retail locations, and security deposits on leases for properties tied to our applications. Additionally, we had to buy out of a signed lease to terminate a convenience store development, which our out-of-state partner had chosen as the ideal location for our cultivation application due to its proximity to I-70 and easy access to major highways. These costs were approximately $1 million, which were fully at risk with no guarantee of being awarded any licenses. While some viewed this as a significant gamble, we believed the potential rewards were worth the risk, should we be awarded the licenses.

We hired a consultant and an attorney, both out of St. Louis, who were experienced in the cannabis licensing process and had connections to investors and operators. This consultant and attorney had an influx of out-of-state operators requesting introductions to Missouri residents to provide the requisite Missouri capital. The consultant and attorney coordinated our introductions to several out-of-state, experienced operators. We interviewed and toured numerous out-of-state operators' facilities to set up what would be my first investment in the cannabis space. After touring several facilities and meeting with several operators who either weren't business-minded or didn't align with our values, we were close to waving the flag on this investment altogether and taking our current loss before we even submitted applications.

That was when I got a call from Dan, our attorney. He wanted us to meet one more time with a group based out of Colorado. This group, Terrapin Care Station, operated successfully in Colorado and Pennsylvania at the time and was building a facility in Michigan. I remember on the call with their CEO, Chris Woods, and Director of Government Affairs, Nico Pento, how comfortable PJ and I felt with the direction they were taking their company and with their growth strategy. They seemed to have an understanding of all three license facets: cultivation, manufactured products, and retail. They also modeled price compression based on the Missouri forecast and had operational data from other states to apply to the Missouri market when forecasting ebbs and flows.

In addition, Woods, the CEO, told me this would be "mailbox money," meaning I would be totally hands-off after the investment and simply walk to the mailbox once a month to receive a distribution check for my investment. This was quite different from all the other investments I had previously made. With those other investments, I knew I would have some level of hands-on work, whether from a financial perspective, talent recruitment, strategy and vision, marketing, operational efficiencies, or growth and development.

I knew it was a commodity-based business, but when vertically integrated, it became multifaceted. Vertical integration refers to a business that controls all stages of its supply chain. In cannabis, that means companies own and control the cultivation, lab, extraction, manufacturing, and retail licensed components of their business. It encompasses agricultural cultivation, production, manufacturing, infused products, packaging, fulfillment, transportation, marketing, sales, and retail, all under stringent regulatory oversight. We can control our entire supply chain from seed to sale, which creates efficiencies, better quality control, and the ability to move quickly and make decisions to pivot based on market conditions.

I found it odd that none of the operators I met in this industry seemed to understand their cost of goods sold or market pricing and forecasting, and it was constantly deviating. All they knew was that their businesses were all growing at the beginning of the cannabis "green rush" and that the first ones to market made a lot of money for a short period of time. They grew through winning licenses in the application process, accessing the right markets at the right time, demand outpacing supply, and, lastly, through other people's money (OPM)! The operators we had met with did not have any real, sustainable business principles.

We felt that Terrapin was different.

When touring Terrapin facilities in Colorado and Pennsylvania, we met with their Director of Cultivation, Ian Peak, who was extremely knowledgeable and had built multiple facilities across the country. We even met with some of their investors in CO and PA, who spoke very highly of the team.

We decided to move forward with our cannabis investment and committed to investing in Terrapin Investment Fund IV, the Missouri investment fund. We applied for one cultivation, one manufacturing, and five retail licenses. I immediately began raising capital for approximately 60% of the company under a company that I formed, Elevate Missouri, LLC. Our portion of this investment would commit close to $9 million of the original $15 million investment that Terrapin projected was necessary to build out our facilities, should we win the licenses for which we had applied. The other $6 million would come from Woods and previous investors from other Terrapin investment funds in Pennsylvania and Colorado.

Due to my previous investment success, I had several friends and family members who wanted to invest in me and in the investments I believed in.

I raised the Elevate Missouri portion of the $9 million relatively quickly, with PJ and me putting up most of the money. Approximately forty other members, including friends and family, made up the difference. The Private Placement Memorandum, projections, and investor deck were created and circulated by Woods and his accounting team. I made sure that our friends and family knew we were relying on them, not me, for the projections and operations.

In late 2019 and early 2020, cannabis licenses were issued to the winning applicants. Our group, Terrapin Investment Fund IV, won three of the five retail dispensary licenses that we applied for in the Kansas City area. However, we were not issued any licenses for cultivation or manufacturing. Our vision was never just to operate retail storefronts. We wanted to integrate vertically by adding cultivation and manufacturing licenses. Controlling the cultivation and manufacturing of our product would give us distribution points for our products, increasing margins for those sold through our retail stores. This approach would eliminate the need to sell all products wholesale or purchase third-party products to sell through our retail locations.

PJ and I had already started building our cultivation facility. We had invested a significant amount of money into one of our warehouses, anticipating winning a cultivation license or buying one once they were issued and available. We also began construction on all three retail locations, all in Kansas City, as soon as our licenses were awarded, aiming to be first to market with retail sales.

It was paramount to our investment that we found cultivation and manufacturing licenses, as all the financial projections were based on this vertical integration.

We were able to purchase a cultivation license from a group that had won three but didn't need all of them, as it would have led to overproduction for their brand and products. They only wanted to operate under one license. Each cultivation license allowed for 30,000 sq.ft. of flower canopy under state regulations. We acquired the license for $2,100,000 and applied for a location change of that license with the state regulatory department to operate at our facility. Additionally, we purchased a manufacturing license for $420,000 to house in the same facility through the same location change process.

The dispensary retail construction was completed before the cultivation and manufacturing facilities, as it was a less intensive build-out. My real estate development background allowed me to be very hands-on throughout the process. We utilized architects and contractors that I had been using for years on other redevelopment projects. This allowed us to manage the budget and timeline. While I learned more about the cannabis industry than anticipated, expedited construction completion was critical to our strategy. I had already been more hands-on than I had expected; I was ready to go to the mailbox and get my money!

To the contrary, problems began to arise with our out-of-state operating partner. Despite our retail completion and commencement with the state granting us approval to operate, the CEO insisted on waiting to open the retail store until they could have their Terrapin-branded products on the shelves from day one. These products were months away from being finished, packaged, and ready for retail. We hadn't even begun cultivating and manufacturing out of our facility. I repeatedly pushed for us to start selling third-party products that we could purchase from other cultivators and manufacturers to drive foot traffic and revenue, and win the first-time consumers, since the stores were already built. It seemed to me that first-movers in the cannabis space, as with any other industry, would come out ahead. It was shocking to me that someone with so much self-proclaimed historical experience resisted this basic marketing principle.

Yet, they did, claiming their experience in other states made them the authority on the matter.

Given my substantial investment and friends and family's contributions, I chose not to push too hard and allowed the experienced multi-state operator to take the lead. However, behind the scenes, I started investigating more into the MO market, speaking to other operators and finding out how Terrapin was perceived in our state. I gained a better understanding of the market and started building relationships with other licensed operators in Missouri.

Prior to the completion of the cultivation and manufacturing facility and well ahead of cultivation operations beginning, we faced a substantial cash call. A multi-million-dollar cash call. As you may recall, we had already secured $15 million to fund this project, based on a pro forma for five retail dispensaries and a cultivation and manufacturing facility. We only built out three dispensaries, were halfway through construction on the cultivation and manufacturing facility, and we were out of money. Now I had to present to our friends and family this demand from Woods without any financial documentation to support it. These were investors who trusted my decision to invest in this company and were now questioning my judgement of the industry and the operator.

We fulfilled our obligation because we knew we were close. We were at the 10-yard line, getting ready to score, but I made it clear to Woods that it would be the last time we would fund a capital call.

Six months after launching our cultivation facility, we opened our first retail store and began selling finished, Terrapin-branded products in Missouri. At that point, we were already behind the eight ball, having cycled through multiple CFOs and never receiving monthly or quarterly financial statements. Once our products hit the shelves, they were sold exclusively in our own stores, with little to no third-party products in the mix. This lack of product diversity meant we had no reciprocal wholesale relationships or leverage to get our finished goods into other retailers, ultimately leading to an excessive buildup of cultivated and manufactured inventory.

Through some of my Missouri industry research, I found that Terrapin Care Station was not perceived as an industry team player. I received overwhelmingly negative feedback on our brands and most of the leadership out of Colorado. Several other operators in the state had told me they wouldn't do business with Terrapin, obviously not knowing that I was a significant investor at the time. I tried to explain to Woods that Missouri is not like other states. It is a *you scratch my back, and I will scratch yours* type of state. The roots run deep here in Missouri, and people want to do business with like-minded individuals, not egotistical narcissists who lack the capacity to collaborate and only point out others' problems without examining their own.

By the end of 2021, sales were grossly underperforming, and the leadership team was spiraling out of control. Inventory was stacking up, we were losing hundreds of thousands a month, the financial burn was ready to cause an implosion, and we were through our cash reserves. We had refused to fund any additional capital calls, especially without financial documentation to show where the money had gone that they managed to burn through. Due to not funding these capital calls, Woods allegedly lent the company over $2 million to the MO operation. The underperformance of the Missouri operation and the inability to produce positive cash flow had Woods continuously threatening to fire everyone and close it down.

By this point, I began to question whether I had chosen the wrong partner, whether he was the right CEO for the job, or whether we should have gotten involved at all. While the company was successful in other states, the leadership was failing in Missouri and had no solution. We requested that Woods hire a CEO and step down, transitioning to just being the founder and bringing in someone else to run operations and lead strategy and execution. He had become unstable and was no longer capable of scaling the company. It was clear that he needed to either sell or step aside.

It wasn't just our company that was struggling; the Missouri cannabis market was circling the drain. In Missouri, few cannabis companies were profitable, with only medical marijuana sales. Most of the other companies that were losing money again had no operational foresight; they simply expected this to be a license to print money, and frankly, it wasn't. Our operators kept insisting we wait for the adult-use market, which meant that any person with a valid ID over the age of 21 could walk into a dispensary and purchase marijuana products. Some projected this would triple the overall revenue of the MO Cannabis market.

Poor leadership and strategy would ultimately lead to long-term failure, regardless of the type of market. Sure, going to an adult-use market could mask a lot of the problems that the company had in the short term when the demand is grossly outpacing the supply, but it would never be a long-term solution when there is systematic failure in the foundation of the industry, economic imbalance, competitive market, and commoditization of the products.

Further overall market research years after our investment into the cannabis industry made me realize that it wasn't just MO cannabis companies struggling; it was the cannabis industry as a whole. The global cannabis stock index, which tracks all publicly traded cannabis stock activity, is down 93.6% since its high in February of 2021, shortly after our investment in this sector.

Legalizing adult use of cannabis in MO would be great initially, but the industry as a whole still faces major headwinds. We still need some level of federal support and marijuana reform.

Access to traditional banking services without paying exurbanite, borderline extortion style fees; tax parity with other like-kind businesses – the cannabis industry is subject to something referred to as "280E taxes" which prohibits cannabis companies from taking ordinary business deductions resulting in an 80-90% effective tax rate; rescheduling cannabis from a schedule I narcotic to schedule 3 – treating cannabis more like pseudoephedrine than heroine! Any one of these changes would have immediate positive impacts on the industry and be tremendous tailwinds. The simple ability to borrow money for growth at market rates would be substantial.

Cannabis companies fund their growth with non-conventional lenders at 15% or higher interest rates, depending on the risk profile; it is essentially legal loan sharking. Something needs to change for this industry to gain traction.

Eighty percent of cannabis companies lose money, and seventy percent fail.

I was able to secure bank access on the backend for our operating company, and it was grim. The latest CFO for Terrapin had stepped down yet again. We were on our fifth CFO and still never saw any financials. It had become clear to me that our operating partner was a Fugazi – in the Italian-American community, that's someone who's all front and no foundation – a fake. Worse than that, they had no humility; they would keep insisting their way was the right way - and, to them, the only way. At this point, I knew we had chosen the wrong horse; there were show horses, plow horses, and racehorses, and we picked a donkey. This race was over.

In January 2022, Woods flew his entire leadership team via private jet to Telluride, Colorado, for an executive retreat. It was not a team-building collaborative retreat, but rather a "Survivor Weekend" to see who would speak up and challenge him regarding the company's direction. If you didn't agree with him and weren't, in essence, 100% submissive to his dictatorship, you were gone and left to find your own way home, no longer able to fly back with him on the jet. There are two ways to get to Telluride, Colorado, via car or private jet; the closest commercial airport is 50 miles away on the other side of a mountain.

Members of the leadership team whom we trusted and who were a major reason why we chose to invest with this group were now gone, fired from Terrapin, in what I have coined as "The Telluride Massacre." You invest as much in the people as you do the company, and now the people who we invested in were either cracking under pressure or no longer with Terrapin due to the lack of clear direction and positive leadership and no longer being in alignment with the CEO's lack of values, strategy, and vision.

Everything came to a head in early 2022, shortly after The Telluride Massacre, as I felt confident that I would be capable of stepping into an operational position. I wanted to put more and more pressure on them to perform or to sell the company. In May 2022, we had an emergency board meeting with attorneys and the board members in my office in North Kansas City, MO.

Woods had threatened multiple times to shut down the company if we didn't square him up for the money he lent to keep the operation going. While we were losing money, he was "lending" the company money and accruing or collecting significant management fees for his oversight.

I had financials from my home health company in front of me during this meeting, and as tensions grew, I stood up and started throwing them down in front of him. Did he know what a profit and loss statement, balance sheet, and general ledger were?! I told him we were not shutting down the company, but said that we would fund payroll through a member loan to the company by PJ, John Campbell (who was an investor in Pennsylvania and Michigan through a relationship with Woods), and me, and then we would negotiate his buyout. He looked at me and said, "Do you think you can do this better than me?" My response was simple: "I know I can!"

When we first invested, we obviously didn't know that our investment with Terrapin would lead us to this point. We also didn't understand how difficult sustainable growth is in this industry; otherwise, we would never have invested in the first place. But now we were in a precarious position, one that I had been in before. Do I lose my investment, which at this point was millions of dollars, along with my friends' and family's hard-earned money, or do I double down on myself and put additional money where my mouth is?

Chapter 9:
Elevate

After days or weeks of posturing, everyone agreed that the best path forward was for us to buy Woods out of the company and for him to relinquish his CEO position for the MO operation. We simply needed to come up with a price that was palatable for all parties involved. We couldn't base the purchase price on a trailing 12-month EBITDA (Earnings Before Interest, Taxes, Depreciation, and Amortization) because that was negative. Our best guess of a T12 financial had us losing millions of dollars. We had determined that the investors buying out Woods would be me, PJ, and John; we had the most initial capital invested and the most to lose.

Besides, why would anyone else want to throw money at an investment that was losing hundreds of thousands a month?!

Most of Woods' shares that we were purchasing were issued through sweat equity because of his "knowledge, experience, and operational expertise," which ended up being bullshit. These were, by way of the prefunded Class B shares, the same class of shares I already held through my pre-licensing capital investments into the company. We agreed to a price, reluctantly, but at this point, it wasn't about the value as much as it was about protecting our initial investment and the investment of those we cared about.

We closed on the buyout transaction on July 7, 2022.

The board now consisted of me, PJ, John, and our general counsel, Chris Frantze. The first official action of the new board was to vote me in as CEO.

"Why me?" I asked.

"You said you could do it better than him," they responded.

At the time, I was still operating a commercial real estate brokerage and development company, finalizing the construction of a membership-driven family social club, and serving as the managing partner of a home health and hospice company. There was no way that I could dedicate the time that I needed to turn this company around.

I promised the board that I would dedicate 20 hours a week to this company, and my pay was structured accordingly. However, during the first week, I spent over 60 hours in the office and at the cultivation and manufacturing facility, interviewing all our directors and meeting with the team. The second week, I spent over 80 hours. As is my way, I was in for a penny, in for a pound. I had three times my original investment in the cannabis space, and now, all my time and energy.

When we announced to the investment group that we were buying out our operational partner and that I was taking over operational control as CEO, I heard a lot of grumbling. The same kind of grumbling I heard with every other business purchase. *What does he know about cannabis? Will the employees respect him? How will he make it successful? He's going to fail.*

One of my first priorities wasn't operational – it was symbolic. We needed a new brand. The Terrapin licensing deal we had inherited was set to expire January 1, 2023, and with it, the last vestiges of the old identity. We still had packaged inventory to sell through, yes, but more importantly, we had a chance to start fresh. It wasn't just rebranding – it was reclaiming the story. We were no longer a struggling company trying to survive. We were building something bold and real. What came next was ours to define.

I engaged The Futures Group, a boutique marketing and branding firm in the Kansas City market, to assist us with the rebranding and to help us build our brand architecture. The name we chose was simple, "Elevate." It was the name of the group I used to buy into the Missouri LLC, and it was everything we wanted our company to be. We wanted to elevate the employees, the culture, the products, the investors' returns, industry perspective, and consumer experience. Elevate Cannabis was born, and with it, a clear message: We rise.

I assigned the rebrand project to my cousin, our Chief Brand Officer, Deanna DiSalvo—someone I trusted to bring my vision to life. Meanwhile, I spent the next few months learning as much as I could about our operations and hiring some of the best talent in the industry to lead our turnaround.

One of my first hires was acutely aware of the uphill battle we faced, but he had faith in me, my leadership, and vision, and decided to join our team despite what other outsiders perceived as a risk. I remember asking him if he was ready to be a part of one of the greatest financial turnarounds in cannabis history. It wasn't something I thought we would do; it was something I knew we would do, and I said it with conviction.

As I mentioned earlier, the cannabis industry is multi-faceted, and we have many departments and businesses rolled into one. Though this was a whole new challenge for me, I was committed to making it work, and I needed my team to understand that. I called an all-hands company meeting.

The all-hands meeting was the most important part of the takeover at the time. It wasn't just about data or projections; it was about trust. It gave me the opportunity to share with my team the state of the company in detail, where I saw issues, pain points, and problems, and most importantly, share my vision and direction for the first time.

No one wants to sit through a boring hour-long presentation of why they should do their jobs. Nor should they believe that someone with no industry experience is going to turn a company around because that's what the vision is. However, this message was to let them know that I had done my research and I was ready for this challenge. Once they saw my growth in a short period of time in my role, I could inspire others to fulfill their potential in the roles they had been given.

Whether I'm addressing the team in a meeting, through a newsletter, or one-on-one, I always make sure my passion is unmistakable. I keep the message simple and clear. And I remind people that they're not working *for* this company – they're building it *with* me. My commitment is this: if you take care of this company, I will take care of you.

A vision isn't something you communicate once and then forget about; it's something you continually communicate and refine. It needs regular reinforcement and updates to your teams on progress. The more often people hear and see the vision, the more likely they are to internalize it. It's a bit like classical conditioning in psychology. These are the marketing tactics used to convince consumers to buy a product. In the same sense, you need to sell your employees on why they should invest their finite time and energy to help you (the company) achieve your goal.

What was supposed to be mailbox money was now the farthest thing from it.

By October 2022, we had achieved positive cash flow, and within a few months, we had transitioned from losing $300,000 a month to generating $300,000 a month.

In November of 2022, Missouri voters approved adult-use cannabis through a ballot initiative. This allowed anyone over 21 years of age, with just a valid ID, to go into a dispensary and purchase cannabis THC products. With that one decision, our customer base expanded overnight. It was a much-needed tailwind—and we were ready for it.

By the end of the year, our revenue was rising quickly. We had one of our strongest months on record, approaching a million dollars in net income, even while still operating under the medical-use model. Then, when adult-use sales officially launched in February of 2023, our revenue tripled. Projections became reality. But we weren't just riding the wave - we were prepared for it.

As a leader, I earned the employees' respect by entering the facility and sitting in their respective departments to better understand their positions and perform their respective jobs. I always encourage open dialogue. Create an environment where open communication and ideas are encouraged and celebrated. People often don't come forward with their ideas because they fear being shot down. The same goes for complaints. It's important for you to take note of your people's complaints because they identify issues that need addressing to help provide your teams with what they need to be productive.

People need to feel like they can express their needs and concerns without the threat of retribution. Implement weekly check-ins to keep in touch with what's happening on the ground and what needs should be addressed. Have your managers or supervisors schedule regular one-on-one meetings with their team members to discuss their concerns and determine the best way to provide them with the necessary support. Not supporting your staff will cost you in the end.

Some studies show that every time you need to replace an employee with a salary, it can cost the company five to nine times their monthly salary for recruiting and training expenses. Average employee replacement costs in America are around $13,996 per employee. This is why a high employee turnover rate can sink your company. You want to keep people on your team who are worth the risk you're taking on them. At the same time, you must do your part to support them in whatever they need to do a better-than-good job.

We were able to retain all director-level employees and above, and our staff from the top down was fantastic; they simply lacked leadership and direction. To this day, only one director-level employee has resigned—a difficult decision for her despite receiving a significantly higher offer from another company outside the cannabis industry.

Even with our rapid growth after I took over operational control, I've maintained a family-owned and operated feel. When I took over, we had one cultivation facility, one manufacturing site, and three retail locations in Missouri. When adult-use cannabis was legalized, I recognized a small window of opportunity before market saturation, price compression, and consolidation set in— based on historical data from more mature markets, I knew this was typically within three years.

We had to act fast; now was the time to scale. We needed to increase the number of plants to increase our harvest outputs while also growing our retail footprint. The simultaneous growth was necessary to maintain a balance of vertical integration. We didn't want to tip the scales to be wholesale dominant because we would be susceptible to the risk of the other wholesalers oversupplying the market and driving the price of the products down, making retailers buy the cheapest product to maintain the highest margin, thus squeezing our margin.

We wanted a balanced level of vertical integration, so if the market did hit the tank, we could maintain a level of sustainable profitability by creating more brands and having dispensary outlets to control our distribution points and move our products with margins to make this a sustainable business while building our brands.

Every day that passed was another opportunity for a new cultivator, manufacturer, or retailer to enter the Missouri market. Another risk outside of our control was a neighboring state legalizing recreational Cannabis, drawing customers away from border stores and threatening overall demand. Eight states share a border with Missouri, and at the time, only one of them had a cannabis program. This was one of the strengths that made Missouri a successful market, but this strength was also a vulnerability. Good thing for Elevate, I make decisions quickly and decisively.

Our first step was to optimize what we already had. By tiering our garden, we doubled our flowering canopy and dramatically increased yields without massive capital outlay. It was fast, efficient, and smart. But it wasn't enough.

So, we acquired another cultivation license and secured a 45,000-square-foot facility near our existing operations. We structured the deal through a real estate holding company and financed it conventionally to preserve Elevate's cash flow. Then we leased it back at market rate, allowing the business to scale without bleeding liquidity.

The goal wasn't to just grow more - it was to grow smarter. We aimed to launch multiple brands, each with distinct price points and positioning, to cater to the full spectrum of consumer demand. Our retail network would serve as the foundation to push those brands, providing us with margin control, shelf space, and a long-term advantage.

However, vertical integration only works if retail keeps up. To match our planned output and give us room to maneuver in volatile markets, we needed to increase retail revenue significantly, targeting $7 million per month. That meant acquiring 10 to 12 additional dispensary licenses.

The state had expanded its license count far beyond initial projections, creating long-term supply risks. At that point, we had just three dispensary licenses to build something sustainable. We needed more, not just for market share, but for control.

To me, the entire Missouri cannabis market is a game of Monopoly™. There was a finite number of game pieces (licenses) and a set number of players who could buy or trade these pieces.

I went on a calculated buying spree, using the $15 million I raised through a Class C stock issuance, combined with $25 million in high-interest debt from a cannabis lender. Due to taking on this high-interest, short-amortization debt, my first few acquisitions had to be performing at a sustainable level that justified debt coverage without tapping into our current cash flow; I wanted them to stand on their own. After that, it wasn't so much about the current revenue of the store as it was about potential. It could be potential at the current location or through the relocation process. I had taken underperforming assets my entire life and created value, and I would do the same thing here.

Many people would question the company's growth strategy and the prices we would pay for dispensaries. There were times when I would purchase a dispensary license, only to buy another dispensary right up the street from that one for what was perceived as an overmarket sale price. I would then turn around and sell one of the licenses and close that store, while requiring the purchaser to relocate the license and put a radius restriction prohibiting them from relocating within 8 miles of our existing locations. This allowed me to drive the revenue of two underperforming stores into one dispensary to create staffing and operational efficiencies, further justify the acquisition price, and create more value for that one license.

I have explained this strategy to other operators to buy, sell, or swap assets because it gave them a greater market share in a certain geographic area. They will then relocate the other license and implement the same strategy I mentioned above, driving all customers to the one dispensary while benefiting from the lift of the other store's relocation.

Some operators understand that the only way for the Missouri market to continue growing is to achieve better geographical dispersion of the licenses themselves. This will enable better access to rural markets and border states, and ease of access will increase the frequency of consumer purchases, increasing overall market revenue. This increased demand is the only way to maintain or increase prices, which, so far, have continued to fall as the supply continues to outpace the demand.

Most retail operators do the exact opposite; they want instant gratification of revenue and aren't worried about the long-term sustainability of their business or the market. They see a store with huge monthly revenue, and they simply relocate a license right across the street from them, hoping to take half of the competition's retail revenue. On the cultivation or manufacturing side, operators are unable to downsize or shift strategy. I don't know if it's due to investor pressure or ego. Operators simply can't bring themselves to shut down parts of their cultivation to reduce supply and maintain pricing stability.

Instead, they lower prices to outprice their competition, racing to the bottom on wholesale pricing to maintain sales rather than profitability. We have seen the same thing happen from a retail perspective, lowering prices to maintain higher sales volumes, even if it means lower overall margins and net income! This stems from a limited mindset that will not benefit them or the market in the long term.

At the time of writing, we operate three cultivation facilities, two manufacturing facilities, and 16 retail stores in the Missouri market, with plans to relocate several for better visibility, access, and drive-thru convenience. In a convenience-driven world, you win by making things easier for the customer. Missouri was just the start. We expanded into two additional states—Arizona and Illinois—each chosen not for hype, but for their structure. We weren't interested in wide-open markets where anyone could obtain a license. We wanted limited-license programs, with barriers to entry that protected long-term value. And we brought our playbook with us. I would venture to say that we were one of the fastest-growing cannabis companies and brands in the country once we took over in 2022.

In Arizona, the flower canopy is uncapped, meaning oversupply had already crushed the wholesale market before we arrived. Cultivators were shutting down, and prices were slowly beginning to recover. We chose to enter lean: 8,000 square feet of high-efficiency canopy, focused on premium SKUs like top-shelf flower and pre-rolls. Shortly after launch, we won the Legends of the Leaf Cannabis Cup for best pre-rolls in the state. We didn't try to be everything to everyone - we just focused on doing one thing exceptionally well.

In Illinois, the market was more stable, with pricing having held steady for years due to a limited number of operators and capped production. We acquired a craft cultivation license that allowed for 13,500 square feet of canopy. We applied the same philosophy: measured growth, balanced scale, and integration through carefully selected retail.

A key factor we targeted when looking for growth opportunities outside Missouri was a program with limited licenses. We didn't want to go into a state where you simply apply for a license and pay a fee to obtain one.

We sought states with a limited number of licenses to help maintain their value. We also focused on established markets, where we could identify gaps in specific product segments and find our place in the market. This approach allowed us to pursue and execute a sound and structured strategy.

We were able to better evaluate the market's ebbs and flows, as some more established states have already seen their bell curves flatten and have leveled out at a price per pound rather than still fluctuating greatly due to supply and demand issues. We aimed to develop relationships in these states that could reciprocate in Missouri, creating a wholesale/retail partnership strategy across multiple states. Lastly, we wanted states that provided ease of access for travel.

This substantial and expeditious growth brought about significant pain points, some of which were self-inflicted. As we acquired stores in Missouri, we did so through seven different acquisitions and prior ownership groups, which resulted in seven distinct cultural and operational perspectives. In the first four acquisitions, we made sure that we had branding and licensing deals with all these companies until we could transition to the Elevate brand.

These transitions didn't go well from an employee buy-in and cultural perspective; the employees saw us as a faceless "corporate" group and were now doing it the "Elevate Way." I also realized that in mature markets such as Arizona and Illinois, the retail partners for which we wholesale our products would be reluctant to carry our Elevate-branded products if it meant their customers were essentially walking out of the store with our branding and marketing for the Elevate dispensary on the product packaging. I also thought there could be some confusion with Elevate Dispensary being our retail name. The customer might think we only carry Elevate-branded products, when we curate a vast array of brand and product categories. I informed our brand and marketing teams that we needed to rebrand our retail operations.

The decision was made, and it involved a three-pronged approach, which I conveyed again through a recorded video message sent to our entire team. We rebranded all our stores to Key Cannabis. First and foremost, we aimed to gain the cultural buy-in and alignment of our retail employees with this vision and message. We are not corporate; we are all starting and building Key Cannabis together. We would delineate our Elevate-branded products from the Key Cannabis dispensary brand. Lastly, this would send the consumer a clear and concise message that we are a dispensary where you can purchase various branded products from cultivators and manufacturers across the state, not just Elevate brands. Key Cannabis does not have a branded product line.

The cannabis industry is full of noise. Tax pressures, regulatory chaos, lack of capital, and unregulated hemp-derived products flooding the market - all of it makes long-term success feel elusive. But in chaos, there's clarity, if you are willing to step back and look for it.

As we continued to grow into a multi-state operator, we needed a solid foundation in place. All department leads and teams are fantastic. We've built one of the most robust brand and marketing teams in the industry. Our COO, Ian Peak, who came from Terrapin, the company we initially invested in, was a significant reason for our initial investment. His knowledge and expertise in this industry are unparalleled, his leadership is unmatched, and the employees would run through a wall for him, as would I.

Our team's growth and development have been paramount to the growth of Elevate and Key Cannabis. We have grown and continue to grow through solid business fundamentals, rather than simply planting a flag because we won a license or because one of the larger multi-state operators was doing so. We have grown strategically by taking calculated risks.

Growth isn't just about moving forward. It's about moving in the right direction. Harmonious growth means aligning your personal development with your core values, passions, purpose, and long-term goals. This is what it means to build a culture. I don't want our employees to think this is a corporate structure; it's family-owned and operated. If they feel otherwise, the message isn't getting through.

It's about focusing on the areas of life that matter most to you—whether that's your career, relationships, personal health, or spirituality—and ensuring that your efforts in these areas are balanced and purposeful so you can always be at your best. You don't just want to make progress — you want to make meaningful progress. Progress is great, but if it's not aligned with what's important to you and what you aim to achieve in life, then progress is wasted. That's time, energy, and resources that you could've spent more wisely on meaningful progress.

My time and resources are now going to cannabis. I am the CEO of a company with 600 employees. I began to identify some of the pain points that I had encountered while scaling the cannabis company, so that I could potentially create additional sources of income horizontally within other businesses while also adding tremendous value to Elevate by retaining money within the cannabis company to further and faster scale that company.

Most cannabis companies believe it's necessary to own the real estate within the company, and many cannabis lenders require real estate as collateral. I considered this strategy and asked myself, "Why would I borrow money for our cannabis company at mid-teen interest rates and tie up company capital in these assets when the cost of capital is so high?" It stunts the growth of my company.

In today's real estate market, capitalization rates range between 9% and 11%. So why own real estate at a 10% return when I can recapitalize that money and achieve close to a 30% return in my business? That math just doesn't add up.

Instead, I can still control the real estate by purchasing assets through real estate holding entities that I syndicate and establish. The real estate company can then borrow money from a conventional lender at a market rate to acquire the assets and fund the tenant improvements through the holding company, amortizing those costs into a lease to our cannabis company.

This has allowed me to grow and shift my real estate portfolio into cannabis, enabling me to keep a closer eye on all my investments while maintaining a steady cash flow into the cannabis operating company to help Elevate expedite its growth. This strategy is similar to the coin laundry but on a much larger scale.

To achieve the kind of growth we've experienced from a structural, cultural, and economic level, you need to be intentional about where and how you invest your time and efforts. It's essential to prioritize what's most important and work your way down the hierarchy. The bottom of that list should contain action items that won't have much, if any, impact on you or your company if you don't get to them.

Achieving success is a group effort—whether in business, family, athletics, or community. I never could have grown Elevate's top-line revenue to over $100 million annually on my own. It required trusting others, aligning with a shared vision, and perpetual improvement.

Chapter 10:
Legacy

"You have cancer."

It's scary to hear those words; it is a scary disease to have to fight. I was with my father when he was diagnosed with cancer at KU Medical Center in 2015. He had just undergone a hair transplant.

When the nurse came in to deliver the news and she said those three daunting words, he exclaimed, "Son of a bitch!"

She replied, "There have been many advances in medicines for treating leukemia and lymphoma, and there are different options you can consider regarding treatment," in a supportive and empathic voice.

The diagnosis of Diffuse Large B-Cell Non-Hodgkin's Lymphoma wasn't the issue. He had already decided that he'd beat the cancer. His main concern was, "I just paid $6,500 for a hair transplant, and now I'm going to lose my hair!"

I have told you a little bit about my dad and his resilience in overcoming obstacles, fires, business failures, and life in general. This diagnosis was not going to stand in his way.

Dad sought a second opinion at MD Anderson in Houston, Texas. Shortly after the second diagnosis, which differed in terms of the type of Non-Hodgkin's Lymphoma (NHL), it was actually Follicular NHL, Dad started chemotherapy. He would fly back and forth from Kansas City to Houston to receive his treatments, and fortunately, his body reacted well to the treatment. Dad went into full remission and was able to ring the bell after a six-month treatment regimen. He was only 59 at the time. His body held up great, and the oncologist expected a lengthy remission.

As much as people don't want to hear those words or go through the treatments, the reality is that a great portion of society does. Every thirty seconds, someone is diagnosed with cancer, and every minute, someone loses their battle. How do you react to it? Different people react differently. My dad remained positive and in an exemplary leadership role, even though he had just been handed this scary news. All I wanted to do was to find a cure for my dad or anyone else who must fight this horrible disease.

Shortly after my dad was diagnosed, I went to a breakfast hosted by a friend of mine involved in the Leukemia and Lymphoma Society (LLS). If you raise $100,000, you can nominate a specific cancer research grant for the funds to support in someone's name and gain access to track that research portfolio. Naturally, my dad was my best friend and idol, so I wanted to fund a cancer research grant in his honor. The goal was $100,000, and I had just 60 days—until the Light the Night Walk in Kansas City—to make it happen.

I sell real estate and own other businesses, none of which provide cancer research or cures, and I don't have the skill set or qualifications to perform cancer research. What I can do—and do well—is raise money and awareness to fund cancer research, providing necessary resources to the experts who are tirelessly working toward better treatments and, hopefully, a cure.

Good thing for me—once I have a target in front of me, I'm unstoppable. The people who know me best will tell you that when I set my mind to something, I make it happen. When the woman from LLS who sponsored the breakfast came around to greet everyone, she asked about my goals within the organization. I told her I was going to raise $100,000. She then approached my buddy Dave and asked how he knew me. He told her I was a friend and a client. She laughed and said there was no way I'd actually raise that much. Without missing a beat, Dave told her, "If Chuck said it, he's going to do it."

I raised $106,000 in just 60 days by leveraging my dad's crisis and tapping into my network of business contacts, friends, and family. In my business, we worked with several contractors and vendors for our real estate acquisitions and projects, as well as vendors in the home health space from whom we purchased medical supplies. These were people from whom we had never asked for anything other than the services they provided, but now it was time for me to ask.

I reviewed our past vendor accounts and the amount we'd spent with them over the last two years. Some of these totals were approaching $1 million. I reached out to each of them, asking for at least 1% of the total value of what we had spent with them. I explained that this contribution would be a great way to say thank you and further validate our relationship moving forward. Almost all supported my request, and many gave more than I asked. They saw this as an opportunity to show their support, proving that if it's important to me, it's important to them.

I also held a couple of raffle drawings. One featured a donated trip to Hawaii worth $10,000 and raised $25,000. Another was for a case of braces donated by my friend Max Weber's wife, who owns Weber Orthodontics. That raffle raised about $12,000.

This was just the start of my philanthropic journey.

I found myself thinking a lot about legacy. Would I live up to my dad's expectations? Would I continue to make him proud if something went wrong and he was no longer here? At the time, I had just had my first son, and I remember changing his diaper, thinking that Bennie might not really get to know the greatest man I had ever met.

This period of self-reflection brought me back to another defining moment, one that forever shaped my perspective on family and legacy—the loss of my grandfather.

As his only grandson, I had the privilege of giving his eulogy. The values of hard work, commitment, persistence, positivity, and loyalty all started with him. He passed them down to my dad, who passed them down to me. I am Dad's legacy, just as my kids and what I leave behind will be mine. People may not remember you when you're gone, but your impact can live on for generations. Even after you've passed into the afterlife, the choices you make in this life can leave an enduring mark, shaping generations to come and changing the world.

In my grandfather's eulogy, I talked about some of the things my grandfather taught me at a young age. He never missed a game of mine—baseball, football, basketball—but while he'd say 'Good game,' he never once told me he was proud of me. Instead, he pushed me forward. He always told me, 'Make money with your head, not with your hands like I had to.' He was a lead mechanic at TWA and moonlighted as a plumber to earn extra money. Back then, bathtubs were cast iron, and this bull of a man would carry them on his back up flights of stairs. He did what he had to do to get ahead, but he wanted more for me.

I hit home runs, threw no-hitters, made three-pointers, broke high school records, and shot a six-under-par 66 in a round of golf. 'That's good. That's great," he'd say. You'd think that was enough. I never gave it much thought until I got married. That's when he finally said, 'I'm proud of you.' When we had our first child, he said it again. To him, that was the next step in life. That was the importance of family. That was his legacy, and one that he wanted his family to understand. He didn't have the means to leave behind a substantial inheritance, money, or possessions, but what he did leave was far greater—a work ethic, values, and a foundation that trickled down from his kids to his grandkids and now to his great-grandkids. The way his legacy has multiplied is unbelievable. All of his grandkids are successful in their own right and strive to be the best version of themselves.

When you reach a certain level of maturity and have a certain amount of life experience under your belt, you learn that life is not only about receiving. Giving has a greater role to play and arguably becomes more gratifying.

It took my father being diagnosed with cancer for me to start my journey into philanthropy and truly learn the meaning and joy of giving back and leaving a lasting legacy.

It took my father's cancer coming back, this time more aggressively and after just a nine-month remission, for me to decide to give even more than I already did. Give more time, energy, and resources to charity, family, business growth, relationships, and right down the line. We are not promised tomorrow, and the fragility and brevity of life should motivate everyone to do more every single day.

As Dad went through his journey, I accompanied him to tests and treatments at MD Anderson. At this time, with the short remission time and the aggressiveness with which the cancer presented itself, the Oncologist recommended a bone marrow transplant. When searching for a bone marrow match, they looked at 10 Human Leukocyte Antigen

(HLA) markers and assured us they would find one on the donor registry who would qualify as a 9 out of 10 match or 10 out of 1o match.

While there, I saw young kids battling cancers like leukemia, waiting for a bone marrow match. They, too, sought a proper match, and I realized there was yet another issue: lack of awareness driving people to donate their bone marrow for life-saving treatments. I immediately signed up for the donor registry, and so did my sister.

For my dad, MD Anderson could only find an 8 out of 10 match on the HLA markers. Because of the 8 out of 10 match, the risk of graft vs. host disease was significantly higher than if a 10 out of 10 match had been found or even a 9 out of 10. The transplant doctor was not satisfied with the options, and he recommended me to be his donor as a haploidentical match because I had one specific marker they needed, and Dad and I had the exact same blood type.

Mom and Dad packed up and left for Houston on Mother's Day in 2017, with the transplant scheduled for May 31. Before the procedure, Dad would undergo what's known as "salvage chemotherapy"—an extremely high-dose treatment designed to wipe out all his immune cells and completely compromise his immune system, bringing it to zero. The goal was to reduce the risk of graft-versus-host disease, where the host cells attack the donor cells as foreign.

The bone marrow donation procedure is tougher on the donor than the recipient. Painfully enough, they poked each of my hip bones over 100 times with a needle the size of a ballpoint pen to draw out the marrow. Prior to the procedure, I flew back and forth to donate my own blood so that, during the transplant and the harvesting of my bone marrow, they could transfuse my blood back into me, using my healthy cells to help speed up my recovery and minimize anemia.

When the nurse came around to change my dressings while I was in recovery, she asked how I was feeling. I replied, "I feel fine." She seemed surprised and asked, "Really? Aren't you in any pain?" I shrugged and said, "My wife is seven months pregnant, and everyone in this building is fighting cancer. You want to hear about my problems?" She just shook her head and said she wished all her patients had my mindset. But that's the thing, isn't it? Mindset is everything—and it's something anyone can cultivate.

The night before I went under anesthesia for the procedure to have my marrow drawn, I gave my dad a letter. Here is what I wrote:

Dad,

I'm going to keep this short and sweet; First and foremost, I want to tell you how proud I am of you; from the moment that we sat in that room and heard the words "you have cancer," you have been strong and positive; spiritually, physically, and emotionally. You have never complained, from the diagnosis to the treatments, the multiple trips to Houston, and now where we are today.

On March 25, 1982, I came into this life, obviously not knowing anyone or anything. You had never had a son, and I had never had a dad, but we were in this together. You taught me how to play catch, shoot a basket, and swing a golf club; the values of sportsmanship, teamwork, and winning. You taught me the value of hard work, and what it takes to be successful. You taught me how to be a man, even though, at the time, I felt like you were harder on me than Andrea, I now look back, and I understand why. You taught me what it means to love, respect, and cherish my family and how precious life truly is. These values that were instilled in you as a boy and through adolescence from Popo, and you, too, instilled in me.

We used to joke all the time about Popo being Superman, about him having nine lives, and alligator blood. Well, that is you now, you don't have a choice; you are his legacy, and you must keep fighting for us, we need you. I have very large shoes to fill in a long line of great men in the Cuda family, and what will my legacy be? It will be my kids; at the end of the day, that's what was important to Popo, and that's what is important to you. Who cares if I die with a bunch of property, a bunch of money, cars, and toys if my kids can't love, respect, and cherish the values that you guys have fought so hard to instill in us? If my kids are delinquents and selfish, then I have failed as a father, if they don't respect the fragility of life and family values, then I have failed as a father, they will carry that on, and that will be my legacy.

The last couple of years have made me realize how precious life is and how everything can change in a matter of minutes. Also, how the true definition and legacy of a man is defined by his kids and his kids' perception of him. Popo wasn't Superman because he refused to die, he was Superman because of the people his kids became, and the perception that we had of him. Well, now you are Superman, we already perceive you as such, and I will continue to do things to make you proud of me, and I will continue to raise my boys into the man that you are and the man that I have become, as they are now our legacy.

If I can be half the husband and dad that you are, I would still be better than most men. But I won't settle for that, I will be the man that you are and the man that you have raised. I love you, Dad; you are the best man that I know.

Once I was out of recovery, they allowed me to visit with my dad. I was lying in the chair getting ready to watch the Royals game, clearly worn out and in pain from the procedure, just exhausted from the anticipation of it finally being over. Dad said, "Hey, bros, you're getting kind of heavy." I just looked at him and had to laugh. Partly because of what he said and partly because I had a painful procedure done, and he was receiving my bone marrow intravenously!

I told him I had a pregnant wife, so I eat every time she does, in addition to when I'm hungry. I had been flying back and forth to give blood and go to appointments with him, resulting in eating junk at the airport. Depriving my body of sleep and exercise more than usual. A simple thank you would have been nice.

His response was, "You need to slow down, I'm just looking out for your health."

Being Dad's donor was an incredible gift. Even more incredible was that we had an engraftment on Father's Day. Engraftment meant that my donor cells had made their way to Dad's bone marrow cavity and were able to survive and proliferate. Life had come full circle—he (and my mom, of course) had brought me into the world, and now I had the chance to give him something of myself that could potentially save his life. His transplant was anything but smooth sailing; there were moments when we weren't sure he'd make it. But through it all, he remained positive. He never wavered, never asked, "Why me?" and never once showed a crack in his armor.

The October following the transplant, Dad was back from Houston, and to celebrate his homecoming with friends and family, we participated in Light The Night—a powerful gathering organized by the Leukemia & Lymphoma Society, where the community comes together to celebrate, honor, and remember those affected by blood cancers. We walked under the team name Cureageous Cuda, and while we celebrated my efforts to continue raising money for LLS, my dad was also honored as a hero that night.

The two of us stood on stage alongside a young child who was also being recognized as an honored hero. I remember looking at that child, then glancing out at my wife and kids at the front of the crowd, and thinking: So many people who receive a devastating diagnosis immediately ask, 'Why me?' But at that moment, I asked myself, 'Why *not* me?' Why am I so lucky to be spared from facing a debilitating and potentially fatal illness? And if I *am* that lucky, shouldn't I show gratitude by giving my time and talents to help others? What if it were me? What if it were someone I loved?

It's easy to live in a kind of denial when we're not directly exposed to the hardships that so many people face every day. What's that saying? 'Ignorance is bliss.' But ignorance isn't an excuse not to lend a helping hand—however we can. I've always prided myself and my companies on being proactive rather than reactive, and my approach to fundraising is no different.

Whether it's helping to spread awareness linked to a cause close to your heart, serving food to people in need, helping raise money for a particular charity, being involved at the grassroots level, or whatever else, what matters most is that you give more than you take.

I always find it ironic that those with the least are often the most willing to give whatever they have, while those with more than they need tend to focus on themselves and hoard more. You'll never see a Brinks truck following a hearse. The legacy we leave is not what we take but what we give—because no one takes anything with them when they go. There's nothing wrong with being successful; don't get me wrong. However, giving and sharing what you have won't take anything away from you. It will add more to your life. There's far greater fulfillment in the ability to help others than in simply accumulating material things. More is more. The more we have, the more we can give.

Put people first, not things.

This applies to both your personal and business life. When you prioritize people over things, your chances of success increase exponentially. Yes, take care of yourself first so you can share the abundance of what you have, but then consider what those around you need most. What does your family need? What does your team at work need? What does your community need? It doesn't always have to be a monetary contribution. You can give your time, resources, knowledge, and advice, open doors with relationships, or sometimes, just pick up the phone to say hello.

I've been involved with The Leukemia & Lymphoma Society ever since that breakfast ten years ago, and like everything else I take on, I've continuously expanded my contribution. What started with that breakfast eventually led to me chairing the Light The Night Walk, where we raised over one million dollars at the event—the first time in Kansas City history. From there, I earned a board seat in the Lower Plains region, led the Executive Leadership Committee in Kansas City, and took on numerous other efforts to support LLS and its mission.

I have since started my own charitable foundation, Opes Charitable Foundation. We've hosted several galas to raise money and awareness for cancer. We also contribute to the Multiple Sclerosis Society, the Foundation for Autism Collaboration and Empowerment (FACE), Next Step (a non-profit organization that makes life-changing rehabilitation accessible and affordable to those living with paralysis), and various other organizations.

Most recently, I had the honor of joining the Dare to Dream Team—a group of influential individuals selected from across the country to raise money for pediatric cancer research. It's a $175 million initiative, and I've committed to raising $1.75 million over a three-year period ending in 2027. All of the net proceeds from my book will go to my charitable foundation, furthering our commitment to cancer research and funding the pillars of the Opes Charitable Foundation. It truly is an honor and a privilege to have the ability and means to help those in need.

Throughout my philanthropic journey, I've personally helped raise over $3 million for this cause, with a total impact of over $4 million. Why? Because I *can*. Because I'm not—and have never been—someone who sits on the sidelines, watching and waiting.

Remember, I told you on my vision board that I wanted to be in the Forbes magazine billionaire edition? Well, I made it – even if it was a recognition of my fundraising efforts and commitment to LLS.

It took my father getting ill for me to get into philanthropic work, and now I absolutely love it. It brings me great joy to use my God-given talents to make a positive difference in some way. It's a lesson I teach my kids: to be less selfish, more considerate of others, and more giving rather than having a mindset of always wanting to have something. I always tell them that if they give something up in the short term, like allowing their siblings to play with something they really want instead of hogging a toy, they'll always get back more than what they give. I try to teach them to put off instant gratification for a greater reward later, to think of the big picture. I mean, they're kids and don't understand the concept of delayed gratification yet, but they know that it feels good when they delay their own need for something. My wife or I will praise them for being considerate of others or allowing someone else to have a go first.

My legacy is not mine alone. Without my wife, Annamarie, by my side, supporting my goals and aligning with my values, none of what I have built would be possible.

As a family, we have been participating in an angel adoption program for years, where we attend a Christmas party with adults who have developmental disabilities and give gifts to a number of them. It's essential to teach children at a young age that giving is more rewarding than constantly taking.

I implemented a program this year with my youth baseball teams, where the kids will volunteer at Opes Charitable Foundation charity events throughout the year. They can bus tables, pick up trash, pour water, hold the door open for guests, and provide assistance wherever it's needed. These kids are 9 and 11 years old, and they need to learn that everything I give them, from the indoor and outdoor facilities, knowledge, coaching, mindset, and most importantly, time, isn't to be taken for granted. They, too, need to give back, and I decided that I'm going to do this with all my teams once they turn 9 years old and get into competitive baseball. This is about growing them outside the lines.

Don't think you just have to give money; give of your time or knowledge. Simply listen to someone, help a stranger across the street, help a colleague when you notice they're drowning in work, greet people with a smile, pay for someone's meal or groceries if you have the means, pay someone a compliment, donate bone marrow or blood. There's so much we're capable of giving if we merely open ourselves up to it. There truly is no excuse for not doing so.

My hope is that you won't wait for disaster to strike before you start investing more time and resources into opportunities to help and serve others.

Some of my greatest successes in the business world aren't profit-driven; they're the success stories of the people whose lives I've helped turn around in some way by sharing my knowledge and giving them the tools

I've acquired to help them be more successful in whatever they take on. It's not just about contributing to the company's growth but to societal growth as well.

In 2019, around the time of the COVID-19 pandemic and shutdown, I began noticing a significant gap in outdoor activities for kids and their ability to engage, develop socially, and hone communication skills. I was taking my son, Johnny, to preschool when we would pass by an old, abandoned 9-hole golf course, complete with a 7,000 sq.ft. building. The building was being used as a rundown workout facility, and the two 18-hole mini golf courses were in poor condition. One day, my son turned to me and said, "Daddy, you should buy that."

I glanced over and saw a real estate sign on the property. At the time, I thought, *what would I even do with that?* I didn't need another project— I was already juggling a busy schedule, and my wife was about to have our fourth child.

But as I started to think more about it, I began to ask myself: What do places like Main Event, Power Play, and Dave & Buster's all have in common? They're all indoors, primarily focused on electronics, and they don't promote leadership, communication, relationship-building, or overall societal development for kids.

What if I could create something different? A high-level, membership-driven social club that would offer the community and families a safe space to develop life skills, build relationships, and create lasting memories together. A place where iPads and cellphones will be forgotten.

I ended up buying the property with PJ Guastello. This property was part of my childhood. My mom would drop me off with my friends to play the nine-hole golf course before I could drive. My grandparents would take me and my cousins miniature golfing, cementing their legacy in us. I wanted to make it part of my legacy.

This project wasn't built with the sole focus of maximizing returns. Sure, we eventually wanted to be profitable, but at its core, it was about making memories. It was a passion project, a legacy project. We began redeveloping the site in 2019, shortly after acquiring it. We touched every inch of dirt and every part of the building, added new amenities, and finally wrapped up construction in December of 2022. Oak Ridge Family Social Club was born.

Now, we have a full-service restaurant and bar, with culinary expertise provided by Chef Tommy Cascone, who, if you remember from earlier, was in CCA with me. We also offer a 20-seat movie theater, a 15-game free-play arcade (I know, I wanted to get people outside, but we needed winter amenities), two golf simulators, an over-21 cigar lounge with a poker table and walk-in humidor, massage therapy/esthetic room, two 18-hole mini-golf courses, 9-hole par-three golf course, six pickle ball courts, full-court basketball court, splash park, large turf area for kids to play football and baseball, stocked fishing pond, party barn for rentals, great management, and a dedicated, happy staff.

We throw massive Fourth of July parties with live music, fireworks, and over 500 people. We host Easter and Mother's Day brunches, magic nights for the kids, trivia nights, cigar and bourbon pairings, murder mystery dinners, and paint-and-sip events, to name a few social events. There's something for everyone.

My vision was to bring all demographics together in one place. If one kid wants to play mini-golf and another wants to play pickleball, they can both come here. If you can't get a sitter on New Year's Eve, you can buy a ticket to our event—we'll keep the kids entertained with crafts in the barn while the adults have their fun.

People have told me they don't want to join because they don't think they'll utilize the facility enough. I say, *That's exactly why you should join.* I have four kids, multiple businesses, and a lot of friendships and business relationships to manage. Now, I can bring all of those components together in one place. Instead of spending five hours playing a round of golf, I can play for an hour, get 9 holes in, meet my wife and kids for lunch, let our kids go play mini-golf while I catch up with a buddy and enjoy a cigar, and the wives can play Bunko. This is what life's about—jamming as much as you can into a short period of time, maximizing every moment.

We originally opened to the public to showcase the facilities in December 2022 before closing it off to a private membership-driven club in March 2023. This was the longest project I had ever worked on, and at the time, it was probably the most expensive project. The response was great. Yet, once again, I heard the mumblings. *How are they going to make money? Who is going to join? How many members do you think they need?* The haters gonna hate. I'm monetizing this with time and memories.

We currently have 360 memberships at the time of writing, which is less than two years after going totally private and closing off to the public. We continue to add amenities, including covering the basketball court and three of the pickleball courts, installing disc golf, and constantly looking to enhance the membership experience in hopes of not only increasing retention but also expanding the overall membership base.

It's so gratifying to me when I meet a new member after finishing a lunch meeting and get a thank you from that member. *The food was fantastic; my family loves this place; thank you for doing this.*

I also use the facility to give back and host charity events.

In the summer of 2023, one of my good friends, Andrew Jones, called me and said he wanted to have an event at the club to raise money for a family whose daughter had a rare disease. Shortly after I got Andrew's call, I got a call from my good friend and former business partner, Frank, wanting to do the same thing. The three of us got together with my cousin Deanna, our Chief Brand Officer at Elevate, who was also assisting with all the charitable foundation events and galas at the time.

Ella-Mae Anstaett was diagnosed with CLN3 Batten disease, which is extremely rare. Batten disease is a group of rare, inherited neurodegenerative disorders that affect the brain and nervous system. It is estimated that there are only 14,000 cases worldwide, affecting 2 out of every 100,000 children. She was diagnosed at 8 years old, and the family's insurance carrier did not cover the medication at the time, which cost approximately $10,000 per month. When Frank, Andrew, and I left that meeting, I told Frank to tell the family that we would host a poker tournament, leverage the crisis with our community and business relationships, and raise $150,000.

I had never met Ella, and honestly, I still haven't to this day. Why would we do this? Because we can, and that's what we do. We were able to give the family $130,000 for their daughter's treatment, and shortly after the insurance carrier saw the medication working to slow the progression, they approved the funding of the medication the following year!!

In just two short years, we have raised over $1 million at various fundraising events hosted at the social club.

Do I want to make as much money as I can? I think that's obvious. However, my purpose isn't to take as much as I can; it's to create and leave as much as I can behind.

As for my children, I have a daughter and three sons. My wife and I are leaving them with the example of a strong, loving marriage. We will give them love, memories, work ethics, skills, and characteristics to be great siblings, good friends, and loving parents. We will make sure that they are considerate and humble people. I hope they see me in the same light as I see my dad, and what it is to be a great husband, father, brother, son, and friend. We are leaving them with the lineage of the Cuda name.

You got it from your father,
It was all he had to give
So it's yours to use and cherish
For as long as you may live,
If you lose the watch he gave you
It can always be replaced
But a black mark on your name, son
Can never be erased
It was clean the day you took it
And a worthy name to bear
When he got it from his father
There was no dishonor there
So make sure you guard it wisely
After all is said and done
You'll be glad the name is spotless
When you give it to your son.

This is the poem my wife gave me on Father's Day.

This is my Legacy.

Conclusion

As we come to the end of this journey, I want to leave you with a simple but powerful reminder: your life is in your hands. A middle-class kid from a family of Italian-American heritage who dropped out of college, developed a gambling addiction, and spent time in jail wouldn't be anyone's first pick for becoming a happily married family man with four beautiful children, a philanthropist, and a self-made millionaire, yet here I am. Rather than letting life's setbacks get me down, I used them as fuel to propel me forward.

The key was in taking responsibility for my life, my decisions, and their consequences. My failures don't define me; they give me the tools I need to do better next time.

The journey from resilience to personal development to maximizing my potential wasn't a straight path—it was a continuous cycle of growth, adaptation, and action. I hope that the lessons I've shared from my life serve as inspiration for you to take control of how you want the rest of your life to unfold.

Resilience is the foundation of not just my story but every success story. We all face setbacks, obstacles, and moments where we question our path. But it's not about avoiding adversity—it's about how we respond to it. By taking personal responsibility for your life and actions, you reclaim control over your life. Every challenge is an opportunity to pivot, learn, and push forward with more wisdom and strength than before.

If there's one thing I hope you take away from the first part of this book, it's that your past does not define you. Your choices do. Whether you're rebuilding from failure or striving for your next level of success, remember that setbacks are setups for comebacks. Keep fighting. Keep believing in yourself.

You are the most important project you'll ever work on. So, make sure to dedicate the necessary time and effort to ensure that the sum of all parts makes *you* as successful as possible. And remember, only *you* get to determine what success looks like for *you*. For some, it might look like running multiple successful companies. For others, it might be the idea of having the security of a job they enjoy that allows them to live a comfortable life. There is no such thing as one definitive picture of what success is. It's a word with very many uniquely individual definitions. Once you know what success looks like for you, it gives you a target at which to aim. Then, you need the ability to effectively communicate what you want (and don't want) to get you where you want to go.

With resilience as your foundation, personal development becomes your framework. A strong mindset, intentional goal-setting, and daily habits determine how far you'll go. Growth isn't a one-time event—it's a lifestyle.

Surround yourself with people who inspire and challenge you. Invest in yourself through continuous learning, mentorship, and self-care. Structure your days in a way that aligns with your natural energy and strengths. Prioritize consistency over perfection because real transformation happens in the small, repeated actions that compound over time.

The principles of execution—time blocking, accountability, and discipline—aren't just strategies; they are necessities. Without execution, even the best ideas go nowhere. As you move forward, take what you've learned here and put it into action. Make your vision board real. Build habits that reinforce your goals. Take the risks necessary to level up.

Although a big part of this book is about my business success, I see that as a means to live the life I really want. True success isn't just about money or status—it's about family, friends, faith, and service to others. It's about building wealth in every aspect of life: financial, mental, physical, and emotional.

The key is alignment. It's ensuring that your goals, values, and daily actions reflect your bigger purpose. When you live in alignment, success becomes sustainable and deeply rewarding.

And finally, never forget that your legacy is built every day. The impact you make on your family, community, and the world around you is the true measure of your success. Give back. Share your knowledge. Lift others up as you climb. Because real abundance isn't just about what you gain—it's about what you contribute.

Vision Board

Just to give you an idea, my vision at the beginning of 2012 included the following:

- A photo of a father and son playing baseball
- A photo of a family at Disney World with Mickey Mouse
- A cover of Forbes magazine, as it was a goal or dream of mine to be in the Forbes Billionaire edition
- The list of top 25 commercial brokerage companies in KC by way of volume from Ingram's magazine book of lists - I needed to make this list
- A picture of a guy ringing the NYSE stock exchange bell after taking a company public
- Men in nice, high-dollar suits, obviously executive-level status, Rolex watches, nice shoes, accessories
- A picture of a Lamborghini and another of a private jet
- Pictures of beaches, luxury islands, vacation homes, mansions
- Pictures of Gordon Gekko from the movie Wall Street and commercial real estate buildings.

These are just a handful of things that I set my sights on achieving, and I have achieved all but one! Anything is obtainable with the right mindset and execution.

References

Ackerman, C. E., MA (n.d.). *Cognitive Restructuring Techniques for Reframing Thoughts*. Positive Psychology. https://positivepsychology.com/cbt-cognitive-restructuring-cognitive-distortions/

Avildsen, J. G. (1976). *Rocky*. United Artists.

Brainy Quote. (n.d.). *Henry Ford quotes*. https://www.brainyquote.com/quotes/henry_ford_145978

DEAR MAN Skill. (n.d.). DBT Tools. https://dbt.tools/interpersonal_effectiveness/dear-man.php

Dweck, C. (2017). Mindset-updated edition: Changing the way you think to fulfill your potential. Hachette UK.

Frankl, V. E. (1985). *Man's search for meaning*. Simon & Schuster.

Ganguly, K. K. (2019). Life of MK Gandhi: A message to youth of modern India. *Indian Journal of Medical Research*, *149*(Suppl 1), S145-S151.

Goodreads. (n.d.). Winston S. Churchill quotes. https://www.goodreads.com/quotes/25265-continuous-effort---not-strength-or-intelligence---is-the

Guest, E. A. (n.d.). *Your name*.

Hartney, E., BSc, MSc, MA, PhD (2023, November 8). *10 Cognitive Distortions That Can Cause Negative Thinking*. Verywell Mind. https://www.verywellmind.com/ten-cognitive-distortions-identified-in-cbt-22412

Holbach, J. (2025). *Hold these 5 'forever assets' to make money in your sleep — Something Buffett says is a must*. Yahoo Finance. https://finance.yahoo.com/news/warren-buffett-says-money-while-150008565.html

Kellogg Insight. (n.d.). *Sitting near a high performer can make you better at your job*. Kellogg School of Management at Northwestern University. https://insight.kellogg.northwestern.edu/article/sitting-near-a-high-performer-can-make-you-better-at-your-job

Kruse, K. (2016). *The 80/20 rule and how it can change your life.* Forbes. https://www.forbes.com/sites/kevinkruse/2016/03/07/80-20-rule/

O'Connell, M., & Kung, M. C. (2007). The cost of employee turnover. *Industrial management, 49*(1).

Orenstein, G. A., & Lewis, L. (2022). Erikson's stages of psychosocial development. In *StatPearls [Internet]*. StatPearls Publishing. https://www.ncbi.nlm.nih.gov/books/NBK556096/

Pollock, D. M. (2023, November 29). *What are cognitive distortions?* Medical News Today. https://www.medicalnewstoday.com/articles/cognitive-distortions

Ramsey Solutions. (2022). *Gazelle intensity: Do you have it?* https://www.ramseysolutions.com/debt/gazelle-intensity-do-you-have-it?srsltid=AfmBOoocYWxwunD1oCU7SwA0nZnROuEE7G65g33jG7yS-VI8_cxDPcXD

Schwante, M. (2024, September 27). *Richard Branson says what separates successful companies from all the rest comes down to 1 leadership principle.* Inc. https://www.inc.com/marcel-schwantes/richard-branson-says-this-1-principle-leads-to-growth-success.html

www.ingramcontent.com/pod-product-compliance
Lightning Source LLC
Chambersburg PA
CBHW071746120626
46550CB00002B/678